Bringing Up
Our Children in
Light and Truth

Currawong Press, an imprint of Currawong House, LLC
110 South 800 West
Brigham City, Utah 84302

Text copyright © 2013 by H. Wallace Goddard
Cover design copyright © 2013 by Currawong Press
Interior design copyright © 2013 by Currawong Press

ISBN: 978-1-59992-886-9

Bringing Up Our Children in Light and Truth

H. WALLACE GODDARD, PH.D.

CURRAWONG PRESS

Acknowledgements

Thanks to the most patient and kind person I have ever known, my dear wife, Nancy. I am amazed and inspired by her parenting.

Thanks also to our children, their spouses, and their children for their patience with me as I learn to practice what I preach.

Thanks to my wonderful parents and ancestors, who planted a love of life deep in my soul.

Thanks to those scholars and friends who have taught me about this important subject.

Thanks to you, kind reader, for your efforts to bring more kindness and goodness to the world we all share.

Table of Contents

Introduction
The Challenges of Parenting

We all want to be good parents. We want to be close to our children, and we want them to develop into good people. We have mental pictures of loving, peaceful, happy families extending from the dinner table into eternity.

But the toast burns, milk spills, chores get forgotten. Children act childishly. And we parents get tired, distracted, frustrated, and overwhelmed. Life burdens us.

In spite of our noble aspirations, we spend a lot of time being irritated with our children—sometimes downright angry. Family scripture study devolves into periodic wars. Family prayers are either chaotic or forgotten. Siblings fight. Children act irresponsibly.

We don't know whether to be angry with the children or disgusted with ourselves. We slump in parental despair. It seems all is not right in our families.

Unless we have the heavenly perspective: "And we will prove them herewith, to see if they will do all things whatsoever the Lord their God shall command them" (Abraham 3:25). The heavenly perspective teaches us that life was designed to be hard. Parenting is supposed to test us to see whether our failed efforts will lead to better attempts. God wants to see if we will learn and keep trying. He wants us to discover that we cannot be the parents we should be without patient effort and His divine help.

After all, He is preparing us to become partners with Him. Our imperfect but wise and persistent efforts on earth will yield not only faith-filled children but reformed and refined character in our parental souls. That is God's purpose. That is godly parenting. This book is intended for good parents who would like to raise their children in light and truth—just as He commands in Doctrine and Covenants 93:40: "But I have commanded you to bring up your children in light and truth."

Two Almas

It had to be difficult being a prophet and leader while having a son who was "a very wicked and an idolatrous man" (Mosiah 27:8). It may have been doubly painful because Alma the Elder was filled with the glorious truth his namesake son rejected and undermined among his followers. Alma the Younger "became a great hinderment to the prosperity of the church of God" (Mosiah 27:9). Alma the son was destroying all that his father was trying to build in his own soul and in the Church.

But the faithful father never gave up. He prayed for his son. He joined his faith with that of fellow Saints, that his son "mightest be brought to the knowledge of the truth" (Mosiah 27:14). In response to persistent prayer, the Lord sent an angel to the wayward son. When that angel confronted the younger Alma with his destructive behavior, the long-neglected teachings of Alma's father came to life: "I remembered also to have heard my father prophesy unto the people concerning the coming of one Jesus Christ, a Son of God, to atone for the sins of the world" (Alma 36:17).

Had Alma's father taught him the true spirit of prayer, or did the Spirit inspire it? We do not know. But Alma uttered the words that changed his life: "Now, as my mind caught hold upon this thought, I cried within my heart: O Jesus, thou Son of God, have mercy on me, who am in the gall of bitterness, and am encircled about by the everlasting chains of death" (Alma 36:18).

Chapter 1
A Model for Godly Parenting

I have commanded you to bring up your
children in light and truth.
Doctrine and Covenants 93:40

We rarely recognize the eternal significance of parenting in God's plan. We may think more about the importance of Church callings. Yet parenting is God's central task: "He doeth *not anything* save it be for the benefit of the world" (2 Nephi 26:24; emphasis added). Parenthood is His core identity. It is His calling. First and foremost, He calls Himself Father.

Earthly parenting is the place where we learn the vital lessons to prepare us to join Him in His work. It is, above all else, an apprenticeship for godliness.

Research has shown that LDS people have distinctive beliefs about parenting, but that their parenting is just about like everybody else's. What a shame that our extraordinary understanding of God's plan has not informed and enriched our way of caring for our children! What a tragedy that our light doesn't shine brighter than it does.

What are the distinctive doctrines that could make our parenting more heaven-like? What are the principles God models in His parenting that should be the core of ours? How can the principles be translated into practices that strengthen our families?

BENEFITING FROM SCIENCE AND SCRIPTURE

God always has the best answers to all questions and challenges. Yet we hardly ever mine His truth for all its riches. I believe science can help us ask better questions, especially in the area of parenting. Drawing on the best thinking of the best scholars can open us up to divine answers we never recognized before. A national project reviewed decades of research and released a report called *The National Extension Parent Education Model,* which identified six principles as central to effective parenting.[1] I would like to take four of those principles—the ones I consider most essential—and enrich them with spiritual perspectives to form a Model for Godly Parenting.

In this chapter I will introduce each of these four principles. I will use the analogy of building a house to help us envision the key ideas for raising children. In subsequent chapters, we will examine these principles in detail and discuss how to apply each of them.

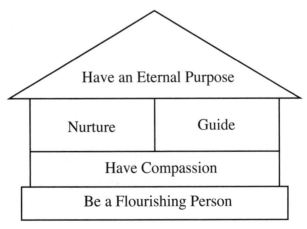

THE FOOTINGS: THE FLOURISHING PARENT

At the base of any substantial structure are the footings. This substantial course of concrete is generally wider than the foundation and assures that the foundation (and the entire structure) will not settle and crack. The integrity of the structure depends on the strength and solidity of those footings.

What are the footings of parenting? What does the entire structure rest on? I believe the footings are each parent's state of mind and quality of character. Parenting scholars often speak of the concept of "parent care for self," meaning a parent must be a healthy, balanced human in order to be a good parent. A miserable, unhappy person is not likely to be an excellent parent. In spiritual terms, when we are not built on a rock, the storms of parenting will wash us away. When we are built upon the rock of our Redeemer, we are solid (see Matthew 7:24).

The gospel of Jesus Christ suggests that we must be converted before we can strengthen others (see Luke 22:32). A corrupt tree cannot bring forth good fruit (see 3 Nephi 14:17). The same principle applies to parenting. A dead tree trunk cannot nourish its branches. A troubled, hostile, bitter parent will find it difficult or impossible to deliver life-sustaining truth and goodness to children. A person who is spiritually alive and growing is more likely to be what I call a flourishing parent, capable of nourishing children and helping them thrive and grow.

Of course, the gospel prescribes very specific actions if we are to flourish. In fact, God provided a clear directive to parents: "Teach parents that they must repent and be baptized, and humble themselves as their little children, and they shall all be saved with their little children" (Moroni 8:10).

13

Apparently it is the process of becoming good parents that is especially apt to help us become good Saints. The foundation principles of faith, repentance, and covenant-making have special relevance to parenting. These are the principles of spiritual growth. We must be good Saints if we are to be good parents.

THE FOUNDATION: COMPASSION

Built on the footings of a structure is the foundation. The scholarly model of parenting recommends *understanding* as the foundation of parenting. This concept encompasses everything from understanding normal development to understanding a child's unique temperament and circumstances. Understanding is vitally important.

God prescribes something even richer than understanding: compassion. While understanding entails a knowledge of development and personality, compassion involves being "touched with the feeling of our [children's] infirmities" (Hebrews 4:15). Compassion goes beyond understanding the child, since it entails a readiness to act in his or her interest. This is best done when we see the world through the eyes of the child. Parental compassion is the offering of our whole souls to experience the lives of our children.

Compassion is exactly what Jesus had as part of the Atonement. Not only did He bear the burden of our sins, but He also bore our infirmities so that His compassion would be fully informed (see Alma 7:11–2). We can never rightly say to Him, "You just don't understand!" He *does* understand. He bore every pain, discomfort, and disappointment any human ever suffered so that He would have perfect compassion. What a terrible price He paid to gain that powerful compassion!

Jesus invites us to have compassion for our children as He has compassion for us. I believe our development of compassion is absolutely foundational to good parenting. In the absence of compassion, we cannot be effective parents.

THE BODY OF THE HOUSE: NURTURE AND GUIDANCE

The body of the house involves two companion processes. In the scientific community we call them nurture and guidance. God calls them something similar in scripture: "And, ye fathers, provoke not your children to wrath: but bring them up in the *nurture and admonition* of the Lord" (Ephesians 6:4; emphasis added).

I believe God chose the words "nurture" and "admonition" very deliberately. These are the exact words Enos uses in describing the godly parenting he received from his father (see Enos 1:1).

Nurture is any behavior the child experiences as warm, caring, and supportive. The key is how the *child* experiences the behavior. In other words, all the parental "I love you's" in the world do not constitute nurture unless the child feels loved.

This is where wise guidance provides the perfect balance for gracious nurture. Children must not only be loved but also learn the law of the harvest. The Apostle Paul declared, "Be not deceived; God is not mocked: for whatsoever a man soweth, that shall he also reap" (Galatians 6:7). Children must be taught eternal principles and the natural consequences of disregarding them. They must learn how to use their agency responsibly.

The reality of mortal parenting is that children won't always feel loved or loving when they are learning the law of the harvest. Sometimes we don't feel loved by God, even though His love never fails. Yet we can create a bond with our children that is stronger than the cords of death (see Doctrine and Covenants 121:44) while helping them learn to honor the principles of eternal growth or law of the harvest. Though God loves us completely, He is serious about honoring eternal law: "I, the Lord, am bound when ye do what I say; but when ye do not what I say, ye have no promise" (Doctrine and Covenants 82:10).

We can best teach children when we ourselves are striving to honor the laws of God. Then we strive to teach our children the very principles that guide our lives.

THE ROOF: ETERNAL PURPOSE

Our objective is not merely to get our children through mortality in a way that keeps them out of hell in eternity. Those of us who have the fulness of the gospel have loftier ambitions. We are preparing our children to do the work God does, and in the process we are preparing ourselves to do as He does and be as He is. That is an exalted objective! In fact it is fully impossible for mere humans—unless we get divine help. When we understand God's eternal purposes, we are humbled. When we earnestly seek heavenly counsel, we are taught from on high, including how to more effectively, compassionately, and wisely parent our children.

In the following chapters, we will walk through each of these principles in more detail, looking at specific processes to help us rear our children in light and truth.

Reflection and Application

1. What parts of your parenting house are strongest?
2. What spiritual gifts has God given you that will help you be an effective parent?

Peace of Mind, Peace in Parenting

It's easy to be irritated when our hearts are darkened. It's easy to be gracious when our hearts are right.

One Sunday at church, I turned to find that our sweet granddaughter Vivian had scribbled in a cherished book. I observed patiently. When she was finished, I added a notation: "Commentary added by Vivi, February 1, 2009."

Perhaps my heart was softened by sitting in sacrament meeting. Maybe it was tenderness for Vivi and her developmental delays. Maybe it was because we love her so much. Whatever the reason, it's easy to do the right thing when our hearts are right.

Chapter 2
Flourishing Undergirds Everything

A good man out of the good treasure of
the heart bringeth forth good things.

Matthew 12:35

It is nearly impossible to be good parents when we are frazzled. Some years ago Nancy and I received a call from an overwhelmed mother. She told us to come to her house immediately because she was extremely upset with her daughter and feared she might do something she would regret. We went immediately. When we arrived we found a tired and overwrought mother and a frightened child. We sat with that mother and inquired about her dealings with her four-year-old daughter. Mom had been pushed to the edge by life and over the edge by her daughter's tiny infractions and normal childishness. What was clear to us was that this mother needed a break. We volunteered to take the daughter for as long as needed for her mother to get feeling peaceful. We expected to have the little girl for a few hours; we had her for several weeks as Mom sorted out her struggles.

We have all seen the effect that stress and exhaustion can have on our parenting. We overreact. We are harsh. We fail to use good sense. We lose sight of the child's motives and needs.

When we're not happy and balanced, our parenting worsens and our children suffer. I believe that being a healthy person is the beginning of good parenting.

One of the many ironies of parenting is that the blessed arrival of children comes with such burdens. It's almost as if God wanted to jerk us out of the center of our concerns and teach us to focus on the well-being of others. It's almost as if He knew we would become whole as we serve and sacrifice. Thus parenting is terribly inconvenient. The demands are relentless and sometimes overwhelming.

One of the biggest problems in parenting is our perception that our children are encroaching on our lives. The reality is that children invite us to a greater maturity and goodness that only come as we surrender our independence, our otherness, our self-serving, our order and convenience. Effective parenting mandates that we surrender much of our concern for ourselves and become more like God—dedicated to the well-being of others.

Life (and parenting in particular) pushes us toward stress, exhaustion, and self-concern. God invites us toward Him and His loving, tender, and selfless way of being. For a person to be a good parent, he or she must be healthy, balanced, compassionate, unselfish, and flourishing. But although this is fundamental, it is not easy for any of us.

MODELS OF WELL-BEING

There are two major models of well-being, one secular and the other spiritual. Each helps us see the path to flourishing. The table below summarizes the secular model as described by Martin Seligman, a psychologist who has studied the factors that contribute to what he calls "authentic happiness."[1] To

Seligman's model, I have added a few scriptures confirming that these processes are rooted in eternal truths. After a brief summary of the table, I will discuss the spiritual model of flourishing at greater length.

	Recommendations for Authentic Happiness	Gospel Confirmation
Pleasant Life	Savor. Enjoy the simple pleasures of life rather than always wanting more.	"Live in thanksgiving daily, for the many mercies and blessings which he doth bestow upon you" (Alma 34:38).
Good Life	Use your talents. People enjoy life more when they take challenging tasks that require them to stretch themselves in using their talents.	Fill the measure of your creation, thereby finding glory and eternal joy (see Doctrine and Covenants 88:19).
Meaningful Life	Serve. People are happiest when they find ways to make the world a better place.	"Inasmuch as ye have done it unto one of the least of these, my brethren, ye have done it unto me" (Matthew 25:40).

Let's briefly consider each of these three levels. The pleasant life is the result of savoring the good things all around us. We appreciate sight, the ability to breathe, the beauties of nature, the richness of friends, the joys of gospel truth. Savoring is the attitude of gratitude.

Savoring can have three time orientations. Obviously we can savor the present moment. But we can also savor our past. What are the good things from the past that enrich our lives now? This may include everything from faithful ancestors to rich childhood experience. The past can provide a rich foundation of well-being—if we choose to find and cherish the gems in our histories.

We can also savor the future. With the eyes of faith, we can look to a future filled with goodness and growth. Knowing that God presides in our lives, we are stubbornly optimistic. We know that even the bad things that happen will be turned to our blessing by a gracious God (see Romans 8:28).

The next level of authentic happiness is attained by using our talents, gifts, and strengths. It is not enough to have pleasurable lives; we yearn to be productive. As we discover our unique strengths, we can design our lives to use them regularly. Maybe your career allows you to use your creativity. Maybe your Church service employs your compassion. When we take on challenging tasks that fit our God-given gifts, our lives become radiant.

The third level of authentic happiness is reached only as we serve. That is the conclusion of solid social science! Service is essential to flourishing. Of course, parenting is filled with service opportunities from walking the floor with a fussy child to being a Scout leader. Yet there is more. When we find ways to make the world around us better, we *become* better. Often, we can draw our children into serving with us. That will help them along the path of authentic happiness.

The best of psychology teaches us to be grateful for what we have, to actively use our talents, and to find ways to serve.

As we do these things, we are more likely to be healthy people who can function better as parents. All of this is in agreement with the gospel of Jesus Christ. Yet this perspective can be enriched and enlarged by considering principles that are even more fundamental and powerful in effective parenting. These principles become clear as we study God's perspective on parenting.

THE SPIRITUAL PERSPECTIVE

We all do things that make our children crazy. In some parent-child relationships, this crazy-making is obvious; the conflict and distance are constant. Other parent-child relationships seem easier, more natural, and more productive. Yet in every relationship we are failing our children in some important way. That is a part of being mortal parents in a fallen world. It is the curse of humanness. In our quiet moments, we know that we're not good enough to properly care for God's children.

There is really only one solution: we must be changed. When our natures are changed, when we have the mind of Christ, when we have had a mighty change of heart, when we draw our inspiration from Heaven, we can be fit parents.

This can be profoundly discouraging, to say the least. We must be godly to be good parents. But we simply aren't godly. We are weak, fallen, and "because of the fall, our natures have become evil continually" (Ether 3:2). The bad news is that "the natural [parent] is an enemy to God [and children] and has been from the fall and will be forever and ever" (Mosiah 3:19). We're a mess!

While our fallenness weighs heavily on us, it is not the only truth about our natures. We are also children of the Divine.

We are heirs of godliness. Our very natures are divine. Glory awaits us.

The Restoration of Christ's Church adds a vital and hopeful doctrine to our understanding of our natures. We are not mere creations of God that can be adopted into His family if we are faithful. We are His seed, His offspring, and His dearly beloved children with whom He is in covenant for rescue. We may depart from the covenant but He never will, because we are everlastingly His.

Let me say it again. We are not simply shop projects to be discarded if we do not hold up well. We are God's children. He is woven into our natures. He will move heaven and earth to rescue us. Thank God for that encouraging truth.

With great truths come great caveats. We must not, like wealthy children who are spoiled, let ourselves feel entitled. We must not think we can coast to ease and goodness. Satan himself is spirit offspring of God just as much as we are. He is supremely talented. But he was and is rebellious. He will not submit to God's plan; instead, he attempts to subvert it.

We are guilty of a related sin when we refuse to "receive all things with thankfulness" (Doctrine and Covenants 78:19). When we protest that the challenges of life are not as they should be, we are suggesting that our plan for our lives is better than God's.

Of course there is one big difference between our sin and Satan's. Satan heard the plan from God's mouth and still declared that he would fight against the plan. In contrast, much of our resistance is due to the veil, which leaves us wondering whether the messy realities of our lives are random and pointless. We commit our sin in partial ignorance. As the spark of faith grows into flames, we suspect that even our aches and pains can minister to our growth. Every challenge of our lives can be a blessing to us.

There is a vital lesson to be learned by comparing our resistance to Satan's. We may recognize that rebellion and resistance send us into bitter tailspins. They send us to the lonely hell of self-sufficiency. In contrast, submission is the key to power. We can, like our perfect example, declare: "The Son can do nothing of himself, but what he seeth the Father do: for what things soever he doeth, these also doeth the Son likewise" (John 5:19).

The irony of it! The most talented person in the world is also the most submissive. The One who might depend most on His own abilities depends instead and entirely on Father. This life is not some random test of submissiveness. Submission is the key to power. "Behold, as the clay is in the potter's hand, so are ye in mine hand, O house of Israel" (Jeremiah 18:6). "Shall the axe boast itself against him that heweth therewith? or shall the saw magnify itself against him that shaketh it?" (Isaiah 10:15; 2 Nephi 20:15).

GOD SUBMITS

Another great latter-day truth is that God Himself is submissive. Three times in the Book of Mormon we are taught that He would cease to be God if He stopped submitting to law (see Alma 42:13, 22, 25). If He must submit to maintain His divine power, how important that we also submit.

Submission is not some random and senseless test of obedience. It is the process to power. It is through surrendering that we conquer. God demands submission of us because it is the key to becoming like Him.

You may ask how submission relates to the command to "be anxiously engaged in a good cause, and do many things of [our] own free will, and bring to pass much righteousness" (Doctrine and Covenants 58:27). I think this relates to a two-stage process of submission. In the first stage, we learn to see His hand and accept His will. This is what we normally think of as submission—having faith, repenting, making covenants, etc. As we become more aware of and tuned in to His will, we are ready for the second stage of submission, where we become active agents of His will. We are indeed anxiously engaged, but in doing His will, not ours. Indeed, we bring our will into harmony with His, so that they are one and the same. This is a relatively advanced stage of submission. Jesus exemplified it. We aspire to it.

Submission is the indispensable, essential condition and ingredient of growth.

WHAT DOES SUBMISSION HAVE TO DO WITH PARENTING?

It may not be obvious how submission helps us to be better parents. Let's turn to Amulek for the answer. The oft-quoted invitation of Alma 34 to pray at all times and in all places neglects Amulek's vital context for the instruction to pray. The point is not merely to pray a lot. Rather, there are two phrases in verse 17 that teach submission. "Therefore may God grant unto you, my brethren, that ye may begin to exercise *your faith unto repentance,* that ye begin to call upon his holy name, that he would have mercy upon you" (emphasis added).

Note the emphasized phrase "faith unto repentance," which is unique to Amulek, appearing four times in verses 15 through 17 and nowhere else in all of scripture. It is a very powerful phrase. It suggests that when we have enough faith, we will bring our tattered, weak lives to Jesus. We trust Him enough to run to Him rather than away from Him. Faith unto repentance is the heart of submission.

The second vital phrase is found in verse 18: "Yea, *cry unto him for mercy;* for he is mighty to save" (emphasis added). In this chapter of scripture, I don't believe that God is merely asking us to pray 24/7. No, He is asking us to recognize our dependence on Him for help with our fields, flocks, responding to our enemies (including the devil), and our crops. We must cry out for mercy in all things. "Yea, and when you do not cry unto the Lord, let your hearts be full, drawn out in prayer unto him continually for your welfare, and also for the welfare of those who are around you" (v. 27).

In order to be godly parents, we need to submit to God on a regular basis. We must recognize our desperate need and cry out for divine help.

- When we are angry, we pray for mercy.
- When we are exhausted, we pray for mercy.
- When we are resentful, we pray for mercy.
- When we are lonely, we pray for mercy.
- When we are confused, we pray for mercy.

We pray for mercy in all situations because, as Amulek observed, God is mighty to save. His might extends to parenting. We cannot be the parents we should be unless we are filled with God's Spirit.

We regularly try to turn parenting into a test of our skills. We're often wondering how to outmaneuver the child or cure this behavior or discourage that tendency. Skills matter. Even more, our understanding of children matters. But no amount of skill or understanding can balance a heart that is trying to operate independent of God and divine goodness.

When our hearts are right, the right attitude and actions flow naturally. As we read in the New Testament: "How can ye, being evil, speak good things? for out of the abundance of the heart the mouth speaketh" (Matthew 12:34).

"Getting our hearts right" may seem like a black box with mysterious contents and magical effects. How do I get my heart right? How can I subdue that natural man within me who gets cranky and contrary? How do I draw the spiritual power into my life that will change my nature? I believe the answer is to do all the things to build a relationship with God that we would do if we wanted to build a relationship with a respected human. Listen. Spend time together. Learn about Him. Show your interest and commitment. As we do these things, the bond will grow.

A key time for building our relationship with God is the weekly interview we call the sacrament. During those fifteen minutes we prepare our hearts with a hymn and then are invited into direct conversation with Him. We ask Him to remove our sins, to change our hearts, and to prosper our worthy projects. We should prepare for such important conversations. I try to take some time every Saturday evening to prepare for the Sabbath conversation with my Heavenly Father.

Every time an awareness of God's power and goodness combines with my own sense of inadequacy, I can have the good sense to cry out for mercy. When I do, God soothes and fills my soul. I find I am better prepared to be a more godly parent and grandparent.

The process of changing our hearts is a gradual one. We get better and better as we more regularly and gladly call on the

God we love. Along the way, we can still parent with love and good sense. We can regularly and steadily pray for an infusion of godliness.

Reflection and Application

1. Do you have a process for cultivating gratitude in your life? Do you write down at least two things every day that went well? What can you do to be more mindful of God's daily gifts to you?

2. What are your greatest personal strengths? You might be interested in taking the VIA Survey of Character Strengths at www.authentichappiness.org. It will tell you which of the twenty-four strengths identified in humans are your strongest.

3. What experience do you have with submitting to God and recognizing your dependence on Him? Will you try crying out for mercy in areas of need—especially in your family life?

For an excellent book on the secular model of well-being, read Martin Seligman's *Authentic Happiness* (New York City: Free Press, 2002).

To Any Who Have Watched for a Son's Returning

By Mary Lyman Henrie

He watched his son gather all the goods that were his lot,
anxious to be gone from tending flocks, the dullness of
the fields.
He stood by the olive tree gate long after the caravan
disappeared
where the road climbs the hills on the far side of the
valley,
into infinity.
Through changing seasons he spent the light in a great
chair, facing the far country,
and that speck of road on the horizon.
Mocking friends: "He will not come."
Whispering servants: "The old man has lost his senses."
A chiding son: "You should not have let him go."
A grieving wife: "You need rest and sleep."
She covered his drooping shoulders, his callused knees,
when east winds blew chill, until that day . . .
A form familiar, even at infinity, in shreds, alone, stumbling
over pebbles.
"When he was a great way off,
His father saw him,
and had compassion, and ran,
and fell on his neck, and kissed him."[1]

Chapter 3
Compassion Forms the Foundation

When he saw him, he had compassion on him.

Luke 10:33

Our own spiritual well-being—our relationship with God—forms the footings on which our parenting structure rests. God is the rock on whom we build.

The next part of our structure is the foundation that supports the entire building while resting on the rock of our Redeemer. I think of the foundation as compassion, which is defined as "a feeling of distress and pity for the suffering or misfortune of another, often including the desire to alleviate it."[2]

We often think we understand the idea of compassion and show it pretty well. After all, we feel sad when our children suffer—especially when they suffer innocently. Yet we generally underestimate all that compassion entails.

UNDERSTANDING COMPASSION

In the parable of the Good Samaritan, this powerful word was used to describe the Samaritan's first reaction to the injured person: "When he saw him, he had compassion on him" (Luke 10:33). The Samaritan was unlike the priest and the Levite, who ignored the traveler's injuries and suffering. Even though it would cost him dearly, the Samaritan chose to embrace the injured man. He "went to him, and bound up his wounds" (v. 34).

Commenting on this great parable, John Welch discussed the word "compassion": "This Greek word is used elsewhere in the New Testament only in sentences that describe God's or Christ's emotions of mercy. As is well recognized, 'outside the original parables of Jesus there is no instance of the word being used of men' (Helmut Koster in Gerhard Friedrich, ed., *Theological Dictionary of the New Testament,* 10 vols., trans. and ed. Geoffrey W. Bromiley [Grand Rapids, MI: Eerdmans, 1971], 7:553)."[3] Brother Welch points out that the word is a "distinctive theological marker" pointing us to God's love or divine compassion.[4]

Clearly, compassion is not your run-of-the-mill pity. It is not even human understanding. It is the divine gift of feeling what another person feels even though we do not have his or her life experience. It is being touched by another person's infirmity (see Hebrews 4:15–16). It is the willingness to personally sacrifice in order to bring healing to someone we love.

The perfect example of compassion is Jesus Christ. In Alma 7 we are taught that He not only bore the terrible burden of sin and death—a burden that would destroy any of us—but went the second mile. He bore our pains, disappointments, and routine infirmities so He would fully understand every pain we will ever suffer. We can never rightly say to Him that He doesn't understand us and our pains. He paid a terrible price so that He does understand everything we experience. So, while being profoundly unlike us in His personal sinlessness, He is perfectly like us because He bore our sins and our pains.

THE PATH TO COMPASSION

Clearly, we should not be glib about the challenge of showing compassion. We simply are not capable of true compassion without heavenly help. Only when we have the mind and heart of Christ can we truly show compassion.

One of the great ironies of parenting is that compassion may be hardest to show to those we know best. Over time we build images and expectations for people we know. We start to think we understand their motives, preferences, strengths, and weaknesses. But we rarely realize that we see through a glass darkly. We see only a blurry likeness of a person. Our own biases and needs block our understanding of that person's heart.

Let's test this idea. Did you feel that your parents fully understood and appreciated your heart? Or were misunderstandings and misjudgments common? For some reason we all tend to think we will do much better than our own parents. That pride—for pride it is—prevents us from seeing any better than they did. We may have biases different from our parents but we, like they, still see through a glass darkly. The remedy for bias and pride is humility: the whole-souled recognition that we do not fully comprehend someone else's life. Only as we stop imposing our meanings on other people's experiences can we be open to their meanings. Only as we listen much better than we normally do can we really hear the cries of another heart. Only as we open our souls to another person can we truly value that person's life.

In my opinion, we can never experience true compassion for another person unless we allow God to open our minds and hearts to that person. This requires great humility and profound faith in Jesus Christ. Compassion is far more than a skill; it is a quality of heart. Have you ever felt an overwhelming sense of love and concern for someone who had once irritated you? Have you ever wanted to lift and rescue an enemy? These are fruits of compassion.

LOOKING INTO THE FACE OF COMPASSION

The natural man is an enemy to compassion and everything godly. By "natural man" I don't mean the rotten, stinking worst of us; I mean the typical person—those of us not perfected by Christ. "Because of the fall our natures have become evil continually" (Ether 3:2). The common parent who runs on autopilot is an enemy to children. One good example of this was given by the brilliant psychologist Haim Ginott.

Daniel, age thirteen, went with his father to a gallery of abstract art.

Daniel: These pictures don't make any sense.

Father: What do you know about art? Have you read any books on the subject? You would do well to get an education before you express an opinion.

Daniel gave Father a deadly look and said: "I still think the pictures stink."

This conversation did not increase Daniel's appreciation for art or his love for his father. Daniel felt insulted, hurt, and revengeful. He will look for an opportunity to get back at his father. From the mouths of our children come words we should never have said.[5]

When we correct without persuasion, long-suffering, gentleness, meekness, and love (see Doctrine and Covenants 121:41), we do not enrich and educate people; we enrage them. The devil laughs and families suffer. Ginott provided another example of an unnecessary war:

> *Kyle, age sixteen, is interested in political science. He likes to talk about strange countries and foreign nations. His facts are not always accurate and his opinions are often overstated.*
>
> *Kyle: China will soon be the strongest nation in the world. Now is the time to declare war on China.*
>
> *Father: Look at my sixteen-year-old military genius! What do you know about such complex problems? You talk like an idiot. Let me tell you a few things about China.*
>
> *Kyle (in anger): No thanks, Dad.*
>
> *Father: What's the matter? The argument getting too hot for you? Well, if you can't stand the heat, stay out of the kitchen.*
>
> *Hurt and angry, Kyle left the living room, while Father went on lecturing to his wife on how to bring peace to the world. Father's sermon on peace resulted in a new war at home. His talk with his son did not create greater love or respect in the family. Kyle did not learn anything about peace, or politics. He did learn to resent his father, and to keep his ideas to himself.*
>
> *Was the battle necessary? Perhaps not. It is never wise to try to convince our teenager that he is stupid and that his ideas are idiotic. The real danger is that*

he may believe us. Applying the rule of not disputing a teenager's opinions, his father could have said: "I am interested in your ideas about war and peace. Tell me more about them." Then Father could have repeated the gist of this son's views to indicate that he had listened and understood. Then, and only then, he would state his own views: "I see we differ in our opinion on China. This is my view . . ." In an argument, the key to dialogue is the willingness to summarize the other person's view, before stating one's own.[6]

THE NATURAL COMMENTATOR

As parents, we tend to vacillate between more and less compassionate ways of relating to our children. Most of us are not unfailingly compassionate. At times we are tender, open, and kind. At other times we are irritable, demanding, and closed-minded.

Sometimes we unwittingly relate to our children the way a basketball commentator relates to players in a broadcast game. From a comfortable press box, the commentator makes a stream of observations. When he thinks a player isn't performing well or living up to expectations, the observations can include judgments, complaints, accusations, and ultimately a negative evaluation of the prospects of a struggling player. The commentator may even make fun of a player who is having a bad day. The commentator makes his calls without considering the players' well-being. When we are far from the action, we don't feel the pain, struggle, and earnestness of those in the middle of the game.

Yet, once upon a time, we parents were the players. Our parents and others were the commentators. We did our best we knew how but struggled with inexperience, fatigue, lack of strategy, and lack of teamwork. Sometimes we were also dispirited by the judgments of the people in the press box.

BETTER A COACH THAN A COMMENTATOR

It is much more compassionate and effective to be a coach rather than a commentator. Admittedly, some coaches can be harsh and insulting. That is not what I recommend. I recommend a coach who is close enough to the players to see the sweat, sense the struggle, understand the pain; a coach who knows his players' strengths and shows them how to use them; the kind of coach who puts his arms around tired players and reminds them why they are there; a coach who provides aid to the weak, holds up the hands that hang down, and strengthens the feeble knees (see Doctrine and Covenants 81:5) with compassionate words of encouragement, hope, vision, and love.

The closer we are to the players and the more we humbly remember their struggles, the more we can be helpful to them. A coach cares deeply about the success of his players.

THE HUMAN FACE OF COMPASSION

Some years ago a Jewish immigrant to America wrote about replacing hardness with softness in parenting. This one-time-schoolteacher-turned-child-psychologist was Haim Ginott, and he taught us about compassion in parenting. I recommend that everyone read his still-acclaimed book, *Between Parent and Child.* (Disclosure: I helped revise this great book.) I share the following story from Ginott:

> *On his first visit to kindergarten, while mother was*
> *still with him, Bruce, age five, looked over the paintings*

on the wall and asked loudly, "Who made these ugly pictures?"

Mother was embarrassed. She looked at her son disapprovingly, and hastened to tell him, "It's not nice to call the pictures ugly when they are so pretty."

The teacher, who understood the meaning of the question, smiled and said, "In here you don't have to paint pretty pictures. You can paint mean pictures if you feel like it." A big smile appeared on Bruce's face, for now he had the answer to his hidden question: "What happens to a boy who doesn't paint so well?"[7]

Contrast this gentle, compassionate approach with those described earlier in which Daniel commented on modern art and Kyle planned foreign policy. Unhelpful responses humiliated; Bruce's teacher educated. That is the difference that compassion makes.

Jesus counsels us to agree with our adversaries quickly (see Matthew 5:25; 3 Nephi 12:25). Rather than being quick to correct, we can find common ground, show compassion, and thus strengthen the bonds that unite us.

As the beginning of this chapter suggests, compassion rests on our relationship with God. When we are close to Him and filled with His Spirit, compassion comes naturally. Unfortunately this is not a very stable state. We may start the day feeling grounded in God, but the barrage of life events conspire to undermine our serenity. Still, the more profoundly and regularly we connect with God, the more effortlessly we will show compassion.

The Prophet Joseph Smith said: "The nearer we get to our heavenly Father, the more we are disposed to look with compassion on perishing souls; we feel that we want to take them upon our shoulders, and cast their sins behind our backs. My talk is intended for all this society; if you would have God have mercy on you, have mercy on one another."[8]

In the next two chapters, I will discuss four kinds of understanding that are vital for cultivating the kind of parental compassion that helps children become balanced adults. I will suggest things each of us can do to make a positive difference.

Reflection and Application

1. Are you willing to watch for pain in your children's faces and be a healer and comforter to them in their difficulties?
2. What pain have you seen recently in your children's lives? How can you minister with compassion?

The Water Slide

Sara is the youngest of our three children. She was always more cautious than Emily or Andy. On one occasion we all went to the water slide. Andy immediately went to sliding, Emily gathered friends, and Sara hid in the car. When I had invited her to come into the water park with us, she set her jaw and declared, "I will not ride the water slide!" I assured her that she did not have to ride the slide but that we would love to have her with us. She came reluctantly.

Once Sara had finally gotten comfortable in the park, I asked her if she would like to see what the water slide looked like. She eyed me suspiciously but took my hand. We climbed the stairs and watched people sit in the tube and shoot down the slide, laughing. We walked down the stairs and watched people shoot out the tube into the little pool. Then we climbed the stairs again and watched people sit in the tube and shoot down the slide, laughing. After uncounted repetitions of the process, Sara asked if I could go down the slide with her, holding her tight and making sure she didn't drown. I assured her that I could. So, once more, we climbed the stairs. When it was our turn, she sat in front of me, I held her by the waist, and we launched. Sara began laughing immediately. Any hint of concern was gone now that she felt safe.

We laughed our way through the drops and curves. When we shot out into the pool, I pushed her into the air. We worked our way to the side of the pool. As we climbed out, she enthused, "Let's go again!"[1]

Chapter 4
Three Types of Compassion

Have ye experienced this mighty change in your hearts?

Alma 5:14

In the previous chapter about compassion, I suggested that this quality of mind and heart is foundational for good parenting and for our spiritual well-being. Compassion is vital. Yet it is also completely unnatural for the natural man. Compassion requires us to extend beyond our self-focused thoughts and concerns. Ultimately, it requires that we get the mind and heart of Christ. Only when we are changed by Him will we be fully and properly compassionate. But that doesn't happen in one fell swoop.

God asks us to do the best we can to be compassionate while crying out for mercy. Godly compassion is the ultimate gift to those who have struggled for it for a lifetime.

TWO HOMES FOR COMPASSION

The Lord taught that "out of the abundance of the heart the mouth speaketh" (Matthew 12:34). While heavenly compassion is substantially a quality of the heart, the mind is the gardener; our thoughts prepare the soil of our hearts for compassion.

When our minds dwell on judgment and irritation, the soil remains hard, sterile, and impenetrable. When our minds understand the unique needs, challenges, and life experiences of other people, our hearts are softened and we are prepared to be compassionate.

Perhaps that is why the Lord used obscure and strong language when He gave Joseph Smith timeless instructions for dealing with people: "Let thy bowels also be full of charity toward all men, and to the household of faith" (Doctrine and Covenants 121:45).

In scriptural terms, the word "bowels" suggests not just our hearts but all our innards—all our feelings, all our insides. He wants more than our hearts; God wants our innards to be packed and brimming with charity.

Then God adds the next condition— "and let virtue garnish thy thoughts unceasingly" (v. 45). When we run into the word "virtue," we moderns often think of sexual purity. It seems clear that God has in mind a broader meaning. I think He is inviting us to look for goodness. "Unto the pure all things are pure: but unto them that are defiled and unbelieving is nothing pure" (Titus 1:15). According to Paul, we see what we *are*. If our souls are judgmental and angry, then our thoughts are cynical and negative. We see badness. If our hearts are pure, we see goodness in all those around us; we choose to dwell on their virtues, strengths, and righteousness.

We are often quite unaware of the one of the commonest ways Satan can hijack our hearts and families. When we let ourselves get angry, our heart rates soar and we prepare for battle. It's difficult to think rationally and almost impossible to have compassion when we have been hijacked by anger.

Plus, when we move into that accusatory mode, the Spirit takes off and leaves us alone; we regress to being the natural man and parent. We say and do things as parents that we know we shouldn't, but we're just too ticked off in the moment to care. This is especially likely when we are hungry, angry, lonely, or tired. We can lose our tempers and feel bad—but we hate to apologize so we try to justify. We set up a system of unkindness and dishonesty. (For ideas on avoiding anger, read the revised edition of my book *The Soft-Spoken Parent* [Salt Lake City: Walnut Springs Press, 2013]; *Anger Kills: Seventeen Strategies for Controlling Hostility that Can Harm Your Health,* by Redford Williams, MD, and Virginia Williams, MD [New York City: HarperTorch: 1998]; or *Getting Our Hearts Right,* which can be downloaded at http://www.arfamilies. org/family_life/hearts/hearts_right.pdf.)

So, God prescribes a combination of thoughts that are upright, holy, and generous, and feelings that are charitable and compassionate. You can see how important this is in parenting. Parents are constantly required to weigh in on children's motives. When our minds are judgmental and our hearts are hard, our judgments will be filled with accusation and condemnation. We become like the great accuser, Satan, who is always looking for the bad and emphasizing it. This is very damaging for children. It leaves them feeling lost and lonely in a hostile world—just as Satan would have it.

In contrast to parents whose minds and hearts accuse their children, God invites us to be like the great advocate, Jesus, who looks for the good in us and whose heart is always welcoming. He knows we will make many mistakes. He knows we will often act foolishly (childishly!). And yet He is prepared to turn those failings into blessings of learning and growth. As God directed: "Let not mercy and truth forsake thee: bind them about thy neck; write them upon the table of thine heart" (Proverbs 3:3). Kindness and generosity are marks of discipleship.

THREE TYPES OF COMPASSION

Compassion is facilitated by understanding, which I like to divide into three kinds, each with a different combination of mind work and heart work.

1. Understanding Children's Development

We can help children more effectively if we understand their development. When we understand development, we are more open to a child's challenges. For example, it is perfectly natural for a two-year-old to try to exercise some independence. The "terrible twos" are a vital developmental milestone. We certainly don't want our children to remain completely dependent on us into adulthood.

Similarly, the churlishness of adolescence is another vital step toward establishing independence. The bold overstatements of teens are the sounds of a growing brain stretching and trying its muscles. When we adults react judgmentally to teens' bold statements, we damage healthy growth. The right reaction involves understanding and compassion.

Some parents might worry that gentle ways of responding encourage brash statements in our children. Actually the opposite is true. Rather than responding to a brash statement with our own brash statement, this approach models mature thinking. It invites dialogue. It demonstrates the kind of open mind that can lead to productive thinking and collaborating.

There are seven developmental challenges that most commonly put parents of young children over the edge: colic, children's sleep problems, separation anxiety, normal exploratory behavior, normal negativism, normal poor appetite, and toilet training. These are not calculated attempts by children to make their parents crazy. They are the normal, expectable challenges of a spirit learning to work with a mortal body in a fallen world.

We can react impatiently and harshly to problems. Or we can try to understand what challenges in the child's world are creating the problem for the child. This requires us to get out of our own life stories and into theirs. This requires patience, open-mindedness, and humility.

For example, colic is inconvenient for parents. In fact, intractable crying by babies is the most common cause of child abuse. It can perturb even a saintly parent. When an exhausted parent is combined with an inconsolable baby, there can be trouble—especially if we begin to think we have a bad child or that we're poor parents. The solution to colic is to be sure the child is healthy, is not overfed, and gets a lot of soothing. There is a reason rocking chairs have been around for centuries. When nothing else works, sometimes a parent must put the baby down and allow him or her to cry. But children do not cry to annoy us; they cry to engage us in solving their problems. They need us.

The bottom line is that most of the annoying or silly things kids do in the course of growing up are perfectly normal. Most of them are markers for children's developing maturity.

Sometimes preferences in style may irritate parents and suggest a rejection of the family's values. T-shirts with rockband insignia, or flamboyant posters on teens' bedroom walls, may annoy us. While it is appropriate to set limits on moral issues such as modesty, we are wise to enjoy our children's growing expression of self. In the process of parenting, we need to be very careful about the battles we pick. Better yet, we can try to see every step our children take as progress toward God's perfect purposes for them.

2. Understanding Children's Unique Temperaments and Personalities

Understanding development requires us to know what is common and normal for children. We also need to understand the ways in which a given child is different from most. We can only parent effectively when we appreciate each child's uniqueness.

Each of Nancy's and my children has been different from the others from the first moments he or she arrived in our family. Emily has always been a people person. Andy has always been creative and enterprising. Sara has always been tender and loyal. All three have wonderful qualities in common, yet all three are as distinct as three different species of trees.

Differences between our children create challenges for us as parents. We cannot develop some tidy formula for raising all our children. What works magically for one child may annoy another and evoke open rebellion from a third.

God knows what He is doing. He wants us to love each child personally, individually, even sacrificially. Some will be easier for us than others. We can spend a lifetime studying our children and their preferences. We can be genuinely open to their uniqueness. We can beg Heaven for needed guidance and inspiration. God aims to stretch us. Nowhere is this more evident than in the challenges of family life.

Brigham Young gave wise counsel to parents. Notice the italicized part in the context of the rest:

> *Bring up your children in the love and fear of the Lord;* study their dispositions and their temperaments, and deal with them accordingly, *never allowing yourself to correct them in the heat of passion; teach them to love you rather than to fear you, and let it be your constant care that the children that God has so kindly given you are taught in their early youth the importance of the oracles of God, and the beauty of the principles of our holy religion, that when they grow to the years of man and womanhood they may always cherish a tender regard for them and never forsake the truth.*[2]

Perhaps one of the best ways to teach our children about God is to be godly with them—to tune in to their needs and preferences and draw them toward God with our love. We cannot drive or compel them to heaven; they must be drawn with gentleness and kindness.

3. Understanding Children's Circumstances

Do you remember some of the things you worried about when you were in elementary school? I remember worrying that I would forget to change out of my night clothes before going to school and would be humiliated to arrive at the classroom wearing my cowboy pajamas.

Each of us worried about different things. Some worried about being picked on by peers or being humiliated by a teacher. The point is that most of us have long since forgotten what worried us as children. That may be good—except we may not realize that our children worry about many things we have long forgotten.

A few years ago a group of scholars provided a list of twenty events to children in six countries and asked them to rate how stressful each event would be to them. There was surprisingly high consistency between children in all countries. Children considered losing a parent to be the most stressful event among the twenty. Given that divorce often wrenches parents from their children's lives, this is worrisome. The next dozen stressors on the list were:

- Going blind
- Being held back in school
- Wetting one's pants in class
- Parental fights
- Getting caught stealing
- Having others suspect one of lying
- Receiving a poor report card
- Being sent to the principal's office
- Having an operation
- Getting lost
- Being ridiculed in class
- Moving to a new school[3]

The events that worried children the most fell into two categories: those that threatened their sense of security, and those that caused personal embarrassment. Of course, there are many other things that worry children; the worries in this list were provided by the researchers and may capture only a fraction of children's real-life challenges. As parents we often don't realize what things worry our children. And we may not realize how often we undermine their feeling of security and even humiliate them.

Years ago some caring and concerned parents asked for advice. Every once in a while their son would go crazy and become a terrorist. Sometimes while the mother nursed the baby, this boy would scream and jump on the furniture. They wondered if something was wrong with their boy.

The parents and I talked for some time and had not found a convincing answer until I asked the mother a key question: "Is there something different in your life when you have these problems with your son?" She sighed and said, "Every once in a while the baby is sick and I spend the night caring for him and walking the floor. When morning comes, I am exhausted. I don't play or laugh with my boy like usual."

The light dawned for both of us. The terrorist son was not deliberately trying to make his parents crazy. Quite the opposite. Once in a while he got up and found that his normally loving mother was a zombie. She didn't talk to, laugh with, or play with him. She seemed to have disappeared from his life. She seemed angry at him. The boy's terrorism was a plea for love and engagement. He was saying: "Mom, what's wrong? Have I made you mad? Don't you love me? Mom! Please come back! I need you, Mom. Please!"

When we see the world through our children's eyes—when we notice their circumstances and struggles—we are far better prepared to respond to them helpfully. Paradoxically, we are often unaware of the ways our moods and well-being impact our children. Our distractedness, frustration, and exhaustion may frighten our children—even when they did not cause it in any way.

These three ways of understanding children are commonly discussed by those of us who study child development. I want to add a fourth to the list. It is important enough that I would like to dedicate a separate chapter to it. So we will continue our discussion of compassion in the next chapter.

Reflection and Application

1. Can you remember things you worried about as a child, or things that hurt or frightened you? What are some of the things that worry, hurt, or frighten your children?
2. What can you do to help your children feel safe and loved?
3. How can you help your children know that God "will go before your face. [He] will be on your right hand and on your left, and [His] Spirit shall be in your hearts, and [His] angels round about you, to bear you up" (Doctrine and Covenants 84:88)?

Seeing Beyond the Silliness

Mrs. Rhea Bailey was my fifth-grade teacher. She seemed to value me as a student. And I loved her for it. On the last day of fifth grade, she gave me a sealed manila envelope and asked me to take it home and open it with my parents. (Naturally I worried that she might have written a note to my parents about the time that I threw Sherry Lee Ball's sweater in the mud as an act of childish love.)

I took the envelope home and opened it with my parents. Mrs. Bailey had cut a circle out of construction paper and had written "Wally" on it. Then she had cut two narrow, ribbon-like pieces of paper and attached them to the circle so that it formed something like a state-fair ribbon. On each of the pieces of paper she had written a quality she thought she saw in me. Do you think I threw away Mrs. Bailey's gift to me? Do you think I thought it was silly? Or do you think I saved it and that it is still in my scrapbook?

Thank you, Mrs. Bailey. Thank you for looking for and finding some good in a bashful, silly little boy.[1]

Chapter 5
A Special Type of Compassion

Touched with the feeling of our infirmities . . .

Hebrews 4:15

In previous chapters we discussed the foundational role of compassion in parenting. Three kinds of understanding facilitate compassion:

1. Understanding Development. Recognizing that many of the irritating things children do are an important and normal part of their development.

2. Understanding Children's Unique Temperaments and Personalities. Recognizing that each child has a distinctive way of navigating life; and, with compassion, learning to accept and value his or her way.

3. Understanding Children's Circumstances. Being tuned into the stresses and demands in each child's life so we can be compassionate and supportive.

You may already see an important theme developing: children do what they do for reasons that make sense to them. Children do not cry in the night because they love to make us suffer. They do not fight with their siblings because they are hateful people. In every case they do what they do in order to survive. Their actions may not be the wisest approach, but they are motivated by some perceived need in their lives.

There is an important corollary to this observation. When we think children's behavior is crazy or irrational, we do not understand them. Our indignation at their irrationality is a sign that we need to stretch our compassion.

Notice how beautifully this truth fits with God's objective of engaging us with each other redemptively. Our feeling of irritation is always a call for us to be more humble and compassionate. It invites us to be open to one of God's still-developing children. This is a test of our readiness to do what He does: offer compassion to strugglers and learners.

So, for me, the fourth kind of understanding that cultivates holy compassion is understanding humanness or fallenness. We all share that desperate fallenness. We all need compassion for each other.

Have you ever felt lost, hurt, and desperate? Have you cried out in the dark for compassion? Have you yearned for someone to pick up your battered and injured soul along the road of life, bind up your wounds, and carry you to healing? I have. And I have been amazed at the compassion Jesus offers me. My stupidity has cost Him dearly, yet He comes to my broken soul, offering His tears and blood to heal my mind and heart.

That is what He asks us to do as we deal with our children who are human and fallen—and childish. This is the foundational task of parenting. It is also foundational for discipleship. When we are baptized, we covenant "to mourn with those that mourn; yea, and comfort those that stand in need of comfort" (Mosiah 18:9). Is there anyplace we can do this that is more important than in our relationships with our children? Is there any better way "to stand as witnesses of God at all times and in all things, and in all places that ye may be in" (ibid) than to show compassion to God's children whom He has entrusted to our care?

PROVIDING EMOTIONAL FIRST AID

When our daughter Emily was in kindergarten, she and a neighbor friend named Donna often skipped their way across the street to the school playground to kick a ball or ride the swings. One day as the two girls left our house and headed toward the playground, Emily stopped at the curb and Donna dashed into the street. A slow-moving car was unable to stop and hit Donna, sending her skidding on the pavement. She lay in the street, clearly injured and frightened.

What is the right parental response to Donna's situation? Would it make sense to approach her and remind her of oft-repeated and wise counsel to look both ways before crossing the street? Would it make sense to tell her that maybe she needed a timeout to reflect on her carelessness? Would we ground her or demand that she apologize to the frightened driver?

Of course not. Such a response would be abusive. We ran to Donna and offered words of love and assurance even as we helped her get comfortable. We called for her parents and appropriate medical care as we provided first aid. We stayed by her side doing anything we could to help her feel safe and to start the healing process. (Fortunately, Donna fully recovered.)

Far more often than we realize, our children are injured by painful encounters with life. They come home bruised, skinned, and bleeding from hurtful run-ins with mortality. We do not realize how often our children feel frightened and wounded. If we try to understand their pains and challenges, we are likely to look at them with compassion rather than judgment and impatience. God calls us to offer emotional first aid. We are under covenant to "bear one another's burdens, that they may be light" (Mosiah 18:8). That is compassion's mandate.

Haim Ginott, the great teacher of parental compassion, tells a story of a child's disappointment—and how a mother could show compassion:

> *When Daniel told his mother that he had been insulted and pushed around by the school-bus driver, it was not her duty to look for the driver's motives or to supply excuses for him. Her task was to show her son that she understood his anger, hurt, and humiliation. Any of the following statements would have told Daniel that his mother knew what he had gone through:*
>
> *"It must have been terribly embarrassing for you."*
>
> *"It must have been humiliating."*
>
> *"It must have made you angry."*
>
> *"It must have made you furious."*
>
> *"You must have really resented him at that moment."*
>
> *Strong feelings tend to diminish in intensity and lose their sharp edges when a sympathetic listener accepts them with understanding. Compassion is a great healer. After emotional first aid has been administered, it is often best to postpone further action. The temptation to teach someone an instant lesson should be resisted. Immediate intervention may only escalate the conflict. It is easier to*

resolve incidents and restore peace when emotions have subsided and moods changed. In emotional situations, a parent's response to his teenager should be different from that of anyone else. A stranger speaks to the mind; a parent speaks to the heart.[2]

Ginott gives another example of compassion. A mother and daughter are cleaning up after dinner, and the conversation goes like this:

> *Dora: I am so tired.*
> *Mother: It's been such a long day for you.*
> *Dora: Yes, and school was so-o-o boring.*
> *Mother: It was very long . . .*
> *Dora: Yes, the teacher is slow. Her voice is so monotonous. And we had her for two periods, math and science, one right after the other.*
> *Mother: I bet it seemed endless.*
> *Dora: That's right. It tired me out, but I feel better now.*[3]

Do you sense the power of a parent offering genuine compassion to a child? Compassion offers children the healing balm of understanding. It also reassures children that their feelings are normal and that the important adults in their lives care about their feelings.

THE FRUITS OF COMPASSION

It is common for us to assume that showing compassion may increase or extend the child's pain. Will the child get stuck in self-pity when we focus on his or her pain? Experience, research, and God say otherwise. When we show heartfelt compassion for someone else's pain, we not only show that others can comprehend that person's pain but also that we are genuinely touched by the feeling of his or her infirmity (see Hebrews 4:15). The child and the child's feelings matter to us.

God Himself sets the perfect example. In the stunning revelation in which He and Enoch observed the suffering of God's wicked children on earth, Enoch was shocked to discover God weeping. Enoch asked how someone as great as He could possibly be touched so deeply—especially by wicked children. God replied, "The whole heavens shall weep over them, even all the workmanship of mine hands; wherefore should not the heavens weep, seeing these shall suffer?" (Moses 7:37).

Amazing! God does not sit in a distant heaven untouched by our struggles. He weeps with us and for us. He asks us to show similar compassion for our children when they suffer.

TEACHING WITH COMPASSION IN TIMES OF TROUBLE

A woman went shopping with her sister and her sister's two children. After several hours, the children were tired and bored. They began to quarrel. The mother, who was rushing to finish her errands, was frustrated by the demands of the day, the quarreling between the children, and the difficulties in finding a parking space on a crowded street.

Then the girl threw a toy at her brother. It missed him and flew into the front seat, startling the mother. As she pulled the car into a parking spot, she yelled at the children, "You two need to stop this right now! If that toy had hit me I could have crashed this car. I am very angry at both of you!" Then she got out of the car to finish her last errand, slamming the door on her way out.

There was complete silence for a few minutes. Then the little girl, her eyes brimming with tears, said in a quivering voice, "I don't like it when doors slam." The adult sister, who was still in the car with the children, said her heart broke when she realized the little girl felt as if her mother no longer loved her and her world was no longer safe.

While we readily understand the mother's frustration, we have to ask if her response to the flying toy taught her daughter a better course of action. This good woman wants to be a wonderful mother, but she left her children feeling frightened and shamed.

It is not acceptable for children to throw things at family members, especially in a moving car. But let's imagine how this mother might have used compassion to handle this situation more effectively. She might have realized that, after a long day of running errands and being strapped in the car, the children were tired, bored, and cranky. She could have recognized that she was feeling irritated and impatient and was in need of a chance to collect herself before reacting. She might have taken a deep breath and invited the children to hold on through the last errand. Or she might have gotten the children out of the car for some lunch and a walk.

Later, at home, she might have sat her daughter in her lap. When they were peaceful, Mom might have offered understanding and helped her daughter learn new ways. "Today was a hard day," she might begin. "You were upset when you were in the car." When the girl felt safe and understood, her mother might probe, "Did throwing the toy at your brother help you get what you wanted?" Mom could listen some more. "Is there anything you could have done differently?" Then Mom could coach her daughter to better ways of behavior.

Compassion sets the stage for effective teaching and parenting. Effective compassion requires us to get out of our own story and step into the stories of our children's lives. Let's consider a couple of common examples.

Imagine that your teenager is working on his algebra homework and groans, "This is so hard! I just don't get it." The instinctive adult response is to say, "It's not hard. You can do it." Now consider the inevitable meta-message we sent to the child: "You think this is hard. It really isn't. Everyone else in the world can do algebra. If you can't do it, you must be stupid."

This harsh message is certainly not our intent. But because we spoke from *our* point of view ("Yikes, I don't want my child to give up—I must push him forward") rather than the child's point of view ("I'm lost—I don't know what to do"), we discouraged rather than encouraged our child.

Consider a different response, one tuned to the child's feelings and experience. "I can see why algebra feels so hard. You are learning a new language filled with symbols and a lot of rules for solving problems. I appreciate how hard you are working to learn that new language." The emphasis in this response is appreciation for the difficulty of the task, and appreciation for the child's efforts.

Consider another situation. A child spills a glass of milk. Of course he or she feels embarrassed, flustered, and worried. What's our reaction? Here are some different responses, some helpful and some not.

	Common Parental Response—Doesn't Show Compassion	More Understanding and Compassionate Parental Response
Attacking versus Solving	"You are so clumsy."	"The milk spilled. Here is a cloth to wipe it up."
Advising versus Understanding	"What you need to do is pay more attention."	"We all spill sometimes."
History versus Here and Now	"You always spill something."	"It's a good thing we have paper towels."
Labeling versus Understanding	"You are such a klutz!"	"Big glasses can be hard to handle."
Futurizing versus Understanding	"You'll never be able to do anything right."	"It's embarrassing to spill milk, isn't it?"

When something bad happens, we tend to be irritated because it is inconvenient for us. We hate messes and wasted time. So we lecture already-embarrassed children rather than binding up their wounds with compassion and teaching them better ways.

We love our children. If another adult were to say insensitive, demeaning, or hurtful things to them, we would do whatever we could to stop that person from having a negative influence in our children's lives. Yet sometimes without realizing it we allow ourselves to be that kind of voice in their lives. The natural parent is an enemy to children—unless his or her heart has been softened by the goodness of God.

LISTENING TO A CHILD'S HEART

Compassion is useful not only when children feel hurt by life but also when they are disappointed, thwarted, or frustrated. Imagine a parent who takes his or her young son to the store. The child sees a toy he wants. He asks for it, then begs for it, and finally begins whining to have it. This behavior could tempt any parent to irritation. "You have all kinds of toys at home, and most of them are scattered all over the house because you never pick them up! I'm not buying you anything else. I don't want to hear any more whining!"

This response is not helpful. Instead, the parent can listen to the child's heart and say, "That does look like a great toy. I can see why you like it. We aren't taking anything home today. Maybe you will want to choose this one the next time we are getting a new toy." The limit can be delivered with loving empathy. And it can be repeated as many times as are needed to convince the child that we are serious. The parent can show that he or she takes the child's preference seriously by saying, "Let's write down the name of that toy. You can keep the note so you will remember which toy you wanted."

Note that the child's whining may also be an expression of boredom and tiredness. The compassionate response to boredom is to find something the child can do: "Would you keep track of the shopping list for me?" A compassionate response to tiredness might be to take a minute to hold the child, to get a snack, or to end the shopping trip as quickly as possible.

As we assist our children in making the journey toward becoming adults, limits must be set. Responsible behavior must be taught. But we can do it with kindness and compassion.

In order to effectively show compassion, we must set aside our own frustrations and irritations. We must desire to understand and have empathy for our child. This is not learned in a mini-class. It is one of the hardest things that humans ever do. It is the work of a lifetime.

EMOTION COACHING

The great psychologist John Gottman has described a process he calls emotion coaching. Rather than react to children's strong feelings by being dismissive, disapproving, or confused, we can teach them to understand and manage their feelings using five steps.[4]

1. Be Aware of the Child's Emotions

Children have reasons for the way they feel. When their feelings don't make sense to us, it means we don't understand the children and what's happening in their lives.

It is good to be aware of special challenges our children may have. When they are hungry, angry, lonely, or tired, children are especially likely to have a hard time dealing with their feelings.

Remember, when children are in the midst of strong feelings, this is *not* a time to talk solutions. Healing must come first. Just like adults, children must be calm before they can think sensibly.

2. Recognize the Emotion as an Opportunity for Closeness and Teaching

When a child is upset, we have a great opportunity both to be supportive and to teach him or her. Instead of wishing our children were never angry or sad, we can use these times to help them develop emotional intelligence. Their strong feelings are also a great opportunity for us to teach and draw close to them.

3. Listen with Empathy and Validate the Child's Feelings

Sometimes we worry that showing understanding seems to endorse a child's thoughts and feelings. Actually, the opposite is true. Denying a child's feelings intensifies them, while showing compassion helps the child manage them. As Gottman says, "Negative feelings dissipate when children can talk about their emotions, label them, and feel understood."[5] Effective emotion coaching helps children to better understand and manage their feelings.

4. Help the Child Label the Feeling

When we use appropriate "feeling" words like "frustrated," "confused," "lonely," "overwhelmed," "fearful," etc., children learn to better understand and talk about their feelings. Their emotional competence and vocabulary grow.

5. Set Limits on the Child's Behavior while Helping Him or Her Solve the Problem

We can understand children's feelings while setting limits on their behavior. For example, when a child is angry with a classmate, we can say, "I can see why you are upset. But we never hit other people."

APPLYING THE IDEAS

Emotion coaching is a way of showing compassion. It is difficult because we humans are wired to react based on our needs. It is a challenge that stretches us toward godliness to pause our own story and listen attentively to our children's stories.

Here are two ideas to help you make the journey of compassion.

- Think of a recent experience when you found it hard to show compassion for your child. Rewrite that scenario in your mind. How might you have offered emotional first aid? How might you have reacted differently during a time of trouble? How might you have listened to your child's heart? Prepare your mind and heart to show more compassion toward your child or children this week.

- I recommend that every parent read and reread one of the great books that teaches compassion. My personal favorites are *Between Parent and Child* by Haim Ginott, *Raising an Emotionally Intelligent Child* by John Gottman, and a book I wrote called *The Soft-Spoken Parent.*

Compassion does not come easily or naturally to humans, yet it undergirds and supports all parenting. Its vital role will become even clearer in the following chapters.

Reflection and Application

1. Have you set your mind and heart to support your children through normal mistakes and misdeeds? Have you prepared yourself to respond compassionately to their pain?
2. As described previously, the footings for our parenting house are our personal well-being, especially our relationship with God. A parent with a vibrant relationship with God is far more likely to be an excellent parent than one who is conflicted about his or her relationship with the Divine.

A Small Act of Love

Terry was a kindergartener. He showed up at school one day with a note pinned to his jacket. He worked his way around the classroom, proudly displaying his note to classmates. Eventually the teacher spotted the note and said, "Terry, you have a note. Would you like me to read it?" Smiling, Terry replied, "Yes, I would."

The teacher removed the note and read: "Terry was unhappy this morning because his sister had a note and he did not. Now Terry has a note and he is happy."

Chapter 6
The Body of the Parenting House—Nurture

A new commandment I give unto you, That ye love one another; as I have loved you.

John 13:34

Resting on the footings of the parenting structure is the foundation, which is our compassion for our children—our tenderness and openness to their needs, preferences, and circumstances. This challenging process draws us out of our own world and invites us to understand and appreciate our children's world.

Next comes the body of the parenting house, formed by companion processes, nurture and guidance. Guidance of children is not effective in the absence of nurture. And nurture without guidance is indulgence. These two processes must be yoked as equal partners.

Most of us are much better at one than the other. Maybe we are good at setting limits but struggle to be loving and nurturing. Or maybe we are warm and loving but find it difficult to set limits and effectively enforce them. We all fall short in parenting in one way or another.

This imperfection should not surprise or discourage us. All of us are imperfect and unable to be what we must be without divine help. Parenting is designed to challenge us toward godliness.

Remember Mormon's command that we must humble ourselves as our little children in order to be saved with our little children (see Moroni 8:10). When we become humble as little children, we become better parents. Learning to be good parents is one of God's ways of making us more godly.

THE VITAL ROLE OF NURTURE

Research is clear about the vital role of nurture. Nothing matters more in helping children become good human beings than being loved and cherished by good human beings. This is one of the strongest and most consistent findings of decades of research.

More importantly, it agrees with the direction we are given by the ultimate parent: "A new commandment I give unto you, That ye love one another; as I have loved you, that ye also love one another. By this shall all men know that ye are my disciples, if ye have love one to another" (John 13:34–35).

The test of godly parenting is whether we love as Jesus loves. Anything less leaves us short of the standard for disciples.

HOW DOES JESUS LOVE?

It is obvious that Jesus' love is extraordinary. His whole heart, might, mind, and strength are dedicated to us. "He doeth not anything save it be for the benefit of the world; for he loveth the world, even that he layeth down his own life that he may draw all men unto him" (2 Nephi 26:24). He loves us completely, sacrificially, and redemptively. He is bound to us by covenant.

You can see the remarkable irony. In asking us to love Him with all our hearts, He is only asking us to do what He has already done for us. In asking us to love our children with all our hearts, He is only asking what He Himself continues to do perfectly. As in all things good, He leads the way.

WITH GOD, ALL THINGS ARE POSSIBLE

If you are like me, you are haunted by the impossibility of the task. I am weak, fickle, and self-serving. How can I love as He loves? How can a fallen human be divine?

The great sermons and examples throughout scripture show us the pattern:

- We recognize His greatness, goodness, graciousness, and willingness.
- We recognize our inability to do as we are required to do, unaided by the grace of Christ.
- We hunger for divine aid.
- We cry out for mercy following the scriptural pattern: "O Jesus, thou Son of God, have mercy on me" (Alma 36:18).
- We continue in faithfulness, striving to make Jesus our co-parent.

Ultimately the only way we can love as we should is to be changed by Christ, filled by Him, and captained by Him—as President Benson suggested. There is no other way, even in the specific domain of parenting. He is the Way, the Truth, and the Life in family life, just as He is in our spiritual journeys.

"Jesus saith unto him, I am the way, the truth, and the life: no man cometh unto the Father, but by me" (John 14:6). And no family makes its way to heaven without Jesus as the Exemplar, Guide, and Support.

I hope this idea doesn't cause you to feel impatient and say: "Enough already. I accept that I need Jesus' help. When are we going to get to the real ideas, the practical tools?" I hope that instead of simply giving this concept a mere "head nod" of acceptance before moving on, you join me in supplication: "O Jesus, Thou Son of God, grant me goodness and graciousness. Give me the eternal vision and the enlarged heart. Grant me mercy that I may show mercy."

Being filled with Jesus is the most practical method of improving our parenting. I'm certain you have noticed that when you are filled with His characteristic goodness, helpful parenting flows naturally from you. I invite you to try the five steps listed above. Make Jesus your parenting partner.

In the next chapter I will describe some of the ways this heavenly mindset will change our parenting.

Reflection and Application

1. Have you felt your need for Jesus? Have you felt His amazing love fill you with joy and spill into your relationships? What helps you to experience that love more in your life? What are you willing to do to make that love a part of every week, every day of your life?

2. Have you tried calling on Him for mercy both in times of challenge and in your everyday life? Will you?

It's Not the Cost of the Gift That Determines Its Value

When I was a high school teacher, one of my students came to me after class and told me how he loved to go up to a nearby reservoir, crawl through the marsh, and watch the ducks. He asked if I would like to join him at 6:00 AM. on the coming Saturday. That time on Saturday morning is usually pretty committed for me (sleep!). But I thought it might be interesting. And I was pleased that the student would invite me to join him. At the appointed time we went and watched the ducks. I enjoyed it, though I am not addicted to it.

A few weeks later the same student came to visit again. He told me that his father had arranged to take him big-game hunting. He had arranged a lodge, a guide, horses, permits, etc. My reaction was "Wow! Big bucks! I guess you are excited!" The student thought for a long time. Then he said, "No. Not really. I wish my dad would go with me to watch the ducks."[1]

Chapter 7
The Practical Applications of Nurture

By this shall all men know that ye are my disciples,
if ye have love one to another.

John 13:35

We all aspire to give and receive love: warmth, caring, closeness, sharing. The modern ideal of love is full of golden light and warm feelings.

But Heavenly Father is not content with superficial emotion. He wants something more substantial, so He gives us families where we are challenged to move beyond gauzy sentiment to real love—love that is lived not only on days when family life is endearing and rewarding, but also on days when it is frustrating and difficult.

Families share limited resources, from apple pie to bathroom time to clothing budget. Because of their many years together, family members are often presensitized to faults and behavior patterns in each other. ("Why can't you remember your homework?" "Why can't you ever put away your dirty socks?") And family members often have a front row seat on one another's greatest weaknesses and deepest humiliations. What better testing ground could there be for love than family life?

MORE THAN FEELINGS AND WORDS

In families, we learn that love is something more than a feeling. Parental love is a commitment to always act in the best interests of the child, even when it is inconvenient. And we learn that love is much more than saying "I love you." Words will not be convincing if our actions communicate something different. In families, we learn that our job as parents is to be the flesh-and-blood messengers of God's love in the lives of our children.

How can we move beyond feelings and words to make love a tangible reality for our children? Here's where nurture comes in. The best definition of nurture is behavior that helps the child feel supported and valued—even cherished.

FOUR LESSONS FROM FATHER'S LOVE

What can we learn about nurture from Heavenly Father? As we study His dealings with His children, we see four key behaviors that can help us learn to nurture as He does.

Lesson 1—Making Time

The first lesson about love that we can learn from Father is to make time for our children. That might seem quite easy for an eternal being, but it is hard for time-bound mortals. In fact, it is a deliberate test of our commitment.

Parenting is wonderfully inconvenient. Children frequently require our attention when we have other plans or pressing tasks. Yet the path to eternal joy cuts directly through sacrificing our time and convenience to bless the little people in our lives. "Inasmuch as ye have done it unto one of the least of these . . . ye have done it unto me" (Matthew 25:40).

I remember when my son, Andy, caught me one evening just as I was dashing off to a Church meeting. Looking anxious, he said his leg had hurt all day and he thought something might be seriously wrong with it. He wanted me to help him, and I wanted to be a good dad. But I felt trapped. I had to go to a meeting. I was tempted to minimize his pain by saying. "It'll get better. It's probably just growing pains. You'll be okay." I even thought about dismissing his concern: "Andy, don't complain so much. We took you to the doctor when you had chest pains, and it was nothing." But I knew those approaches would not help. In desperation I said, "Andy, I am going to a meeting. It wont last long. May I pick you up afterward? We will go out for dessert and talk about it. Is that all right?" He readily agreed.

After the meeting, I dashed home, picked up Andy, and took him to a restaurant. We ate dessert and played tic-tac-toe on the paper placemats. We talked. And his leg didn't hurt anymore. I am not saying the leg pain was invented. I am saying that many of life's pains will pass without crisis when we feel loved. And our children feel loved when we make time for them.

Lesson 2—The Power of Listening

The second lesson of Heavenly Father's example of loving is that He listens. He does not prepare His retort as we talk. He does not argue about our logic or about the facts of the case. He just listens. And He patiently waits until we have gotten it all out. He gives us His full attention. Listening is a great gift of love. And when we add gentle understanding, the gift is celestial.

I think of the boy who arrived home from school sullen and angry. When his mother asked him what was wrong, he said,

"Nothing." (As parents we may also be tempted to protest, "You think you had a bad day? Let me tell you about mine!" This is not listening. It is not an effective way to communicate compassion.) Later his mother tried again. "You seem upset, Son." The son glowered, then exploded, "At school today the teacher yelled at me, blamed me for stuff I didn't do, and called me names."

What would be your reaction if the boy were your son? Parents commonly have one of two reactions. They blame the bus driver ("No one will treat my son that way!"), or they blame the child ("Why are you always getting in trouble? You make me crazy!"). In both responses, the parents immediately focus on their own reaction to what the child has said. In both cases the parents process the situation and decide who is to blame. Neither response helps the child because neither helps him or her to feel heard and understood.

The son has just expressed anger and pain over his humiliation. He needs healing compassion. "Ouch, Son. It must have hurt to be humiliated in front of your friends. You probably felt embarrassed and angry." The willingness "to mourn with those that mourn; yea, and comfort those that stand in need of comfort" (Mosiah 18:9) is the way we "stand as witnesses of God at all times and in all things, and in all places" (ibid). Father comforts. He invites us to do the same for His burdened children.

Some parents may worry that such understanding endorses the son's behavior. "What if he really was a troublemaker on the bus? He needs to be accountable for his behavior!"

Accountability is a true principle, but so is compassion. There is a way to reconcile the two. First we listen, understand,

and mourn with him. This sends a clear message: "I care about your feelings. I want to understand. You are important to me." *After* that message has been understood, after the boy feels peaceful again, a sensitive parent may say, "Son, that was a very hard experience. Can you think of anything you can do to be sure it doesn't happen again?" Maybe he needs to sit with different friends on the bus. Maybe he needs to avoid certain behaviors that annoy the driver. Maybe he needs to talk to the driver about bus-riding expectations. The boy can probably think of some wise and sensible ideas to prevent further trouble. But before he can think of solutions, healing needs to take place. And the wise parent heals with listening and understanding.

Lesson 3—Customizing Messages

The third way Heavenly Father shows us love is by customizing messages to our unique natures. He speaks to each of us in our own language.

Scott is an earnest Latter-day Saint who is looking for peace and insight in his life. Father gives him peace and insight. Nancy is looking for opportunities to serve. Father gives her beloved friends who need her. Wally is looking for joy. Joy is what he consistently finds. "Every man heard them speak in his own language" (Acts 2:6). Nephi observed that God "speaketh unto men according to their language, unto their understanding" (2 Nephi 31:3).

In this world, people's exchanges of love can often be organized into three groups: telling, showing, and touching. For some people it is critically important to hear the words "I love you" (telling). Some people feel loved most strongly when someone does something for them—serving them or investing in the relationship with them (showing). There are people who love to cuddle, hold hands, and be close (touching). Most of us, and our children, want some combination of the three methods.

How can we design messages for each of our children that will be more effective in conveying our love? We can ask them what things help them feel loved. We can also notice those things that seem most effective. Usually, for each child the language is different.

Customizing our messages does not free us from investing significant time with our children. We do both. We invest time but we do it in wise ways that fit our children's preferences. Andy valued mountain biking together. It was important to Emily that we take interest in her craft projects. Sara cherished peaceful walks together. Each child requires us to make time to be with him or her in a unique, customized way. To nurture more effectively, we should follow Father's example and tailor our messages of love for each of our children.

Lesson 4—Making Allowance for Growth and Learning

Fourth, because of Heavenly Father's love, He sees beyond our mistakes. When Moses refused to believe that Father could fill his mouth, He did not berate or give up on Moses. He gave him Aaron. Even after Peter had been so shamefully irresolute, Father drew him up to lead the ancient Church.

If we are to be effective as parents, we must make allowances for our children's growth and learning. They need us to see beyond their unskilled efforts to their earnest efforts.

Some parents worry about spoiling their children with too much support, encouragement, and love. But love is different from indulgence, and I suspect no one was ever spoiled by too much love. We can teach, guide, and hold children accountable while still reassuring them that they are deeply loved and valued.

There are times when being loving is especially hard. Nancy and I learned a powerful lesson about love with one of our teenage foster children. She regularly argued with us and often lied to us. We repeatedly felt irritated with her, which made it very hard to react to her helpfully. But we learned that even when we were irritated, we could ask ourselves, "What would we do IF we really loved her?" We learned to act on a gracious concern even when we did not feel loving. It helped us make kinder, wiser decisions in our relationships with her in spite of her challenging behavior.

The next time your child makes mistakes or behaves in a challenging manner, you can consider, "How would I react if I really loved this child in this moment?" Seeing beyond that moment to your child's earnest heart will help you teach and correct in a way that causes your child to feel safe in your love and guidance.

A HIGHER KIND OF LOVE

Taking time, listening, customizing messages, and seeing beyond mistakes are vital ways to nurture our children. But ultimately there is a higher kind of love. It is called charity, the pure love of Christ. It is a divine gift.

"Love one another *as I have loved you*" (John 13:34; emphasis added) is His command. We are literally to love as He does, but maybe charity is not possible for mere mortals unaided by Heaven. It is, after all, divine love. And only when we are filled with Christ do we love as He does.

Family is a great testing ground. We may learn the fundamentals of love and nurture in our families, but when our kindness and patience are stretched beyond our puny capacities, we must call out for heavenly help. Among other things, family life can teach us our desperate, constant need for God's example, teachings, and sustaining power.

Reflection and Application

1. Think of each of your children. How does each prefer to be loved? How does each like to spend time with you?

2. How can you better customize your messages of love for each of your children? Make a plan and try it out. Adapt it as you learn and your child changes.

Empty Words

One morning a mother was loading her several little children into the car to go to the store. Just as she got them all in the car, the neighbor came over to talk to her. As the two women talked, the children became restless. One of the boys began to climb out the car window. The mother yelled for him to get back in the car. Then she returned to talking with the neighbor.

Did the boy get back in the car? No. He continued to climb out the window. A few minutes later the mother turned and yelled again for him to get back in the car and threatened to spank him. He sat still while his mother yelled at him, but as soon as she returned to talking, he climbed out the window onto the hood of the car. When the mother spotted the boy on the hood, she yelled, "I have told you for the last time . . ." She glared at him but still did nothing.

This boy had learned that parents yell a lot but do not really mean what they say. The bottom line is that threats insult children but they do not teach them. They also don't create real limits.[1]

Chapter 8
Guidance—The Companion Principle

Whatsoever a man soweth, that shall he also reap.

Galatians 6:7

Latter-day Saints have a unique view of law. For us, law is not a quirky and mysterious invention God uses to test His creation. Rather, we understand that law governs the universe, and that God Himself obeys it. According to our doctrine, if He violated law, He would cease to be God (see Alma 42:13, 22, 25; Mormon 9:19). So God is not only a lawgiver, He is also a law follower. His very example teaches us that we should take law very seriously.

LAW AND PARENTING

But there is more to God's example. While He faithfully honors law, He is also willing to make every sacrifice to advance His children's development and glory. Rather than allow the law of justice to skewer us, He provides the sacrifice of His Beloved Son to satisfy that law. His doing so activates the law of mercy in our interest. While being perfectly submissive to law, God is also perfectly redemptive.

What an example God is for mortal parents. While we must teach our children to honor law, we must never allow justice to rob mercy, or mercy to rob justice. It is clear that the dilemmas of parenting stretch us to appreciate God's perfect plan.

Most parents tend to excel at one or the other—love or law. Most of us neglect one while overemphasizing the other. It is not uncommon for parents to polarize across this difference. Often fathers insist that children must learn responsibility, while mothers plead for mercy and compassion.

It is a serious mistake to make law and love into enemies. We should follow God's example by honoring both love and law. This requires more than the wisdom of Solomon; it demands the inspiration of Heaven.

TEACHING A RESPECT FOR LAW

God has declared: "There is a law, irrevocably decreed in heaven before the foundations of this world, upon which all blessings are predicated— And when we obtain any blessing from God, it is by obedience to that law upon which it is predicated" (Doctrine and Covenants 130:20–21).

This is a vital lesson for parents to teach and children to learn. As an example of the challenge to honor both love and law, my wife, Nancy, observed an overwhelmed single mother trying to get her son to eat his dinner. He threw his beans on the floor. Mom was frustrated with him and offered him a hot dog. He threw that on the floor. Exasperated, Mom declared, "Okay! I'll give you a candy bar and you can be sick."

What did that little boy learn? He learned that his own preferences can defeat his mother's wisdom. He learned that his own will can govern in his world. He learned that terrorism pays. These are not lessons that prepare him for healthy adulthood and joy in eternity.

Most of us have fallen into similar traps. At the grocery store, a child may ask for a candy bar. We want to be sensitive to the child, but a nagging voice tells us that a candy bar is not a good nutritional choice, especially just before dinner. The child ups the ante: "I want a candy bar!" We hate to cave in, but we also want to get our shopping done peacefully. Often we try to reason—"We'll be home and have dinner in only half an hour." Sensing that his or her drip torture is working on us, the child shouts, "I'm hungry! I want candy now!" We can't decide whether to be angry or to accommodate. The child pushes—"You gave a candy bar to Molly when you took her to the store." Many of us, for the sake of peace, cave in. We grudgingly grab a candy bar for the child. Our conscience groans at our concession, but we don't know what else to do.

In the Doctrine and Covenants, we read: "That which breaketh a law, and abideth not by law, but seeketh to become a law unto itself, and willeth to abide in sin, and altogether abideth in sin, cannot be sanctified by law, neither by mercy, justice, nor judgment. Therefore, they must remain filthy still" (88:35). That's pretty strong language! While young children do not "altogether abide in sin," we sense that ignoring reasonable limits is not good for their souls.

So how do we set reasonable limits, while at the same time show love and compassion? How do we reconcile law and love, limits and nurture?

1. Set Clear Limits and Follow Them Consistently

When we took our young children to the store, we faced the same dilemma all parents face. We were hurried and harried, and the children were tired and bored. They begged for candy.

But we knew that surrendering to their demands in order to keep the peace would guarantee an ongoing war. It would teach our children that by continually whining and begging, they could override the limits that wisdom recommends.

We told our young children that we would never in the course of their mortal sojourns buy them a candy bar to be eaten while in the store. We were willing to buy them a unit-priced piece of fruit or a box of animal cookies. But we would never buy them a candy bar for in-store consumption. And we stuck to that rule.

Some would argue that our rule was arbitrary. They are right. Animal cookies are not necessarily nutritionally superior to candy bars. But that misses the point. The point is for the child to feel respected while experiencing sensible limits. Your rule might be that the child can have up to three ounces of any treat he or she likes. Or your rule may be that the child can have raisins or dried fruit. What matters is that you set a limit that makes sense to you and apply it consistently.

In fact, many of our rules, unlike God's, will seem somewhat arbitrary. There is no scriptural mandate restricting cookies from living rooms, requiring that piano practicing be done before dinner, or demanding that young children be in bed by 8:30. But some arbitrariness is okay. What matters is that things are done in "wisdom and order," and that children learn to respect law.

One of the most important mottos we developed as parents is related to this point: "It is our job as parents to help children get what they want in a way we feel good about." In other words, we honor their preferences, but within the bounds set by wise and loving parents. This approach can move love and limits from endless and divisive brawling into beautiful and growth-promoting harmony.

There should be a sensible (if not scriptural) basis for family rules. We should be able to articulate reasons for rules—though wise parents know it is futile to discuss the rationale behind rules when children are angry or combative. There are times when endless "Why" questions are children's terrorist tactics intended to keeps us off balance. We should discuss the rationale behind rules when our children really want to understand our reasons rather than argue about them.

There are also times when rules and limits are negotiated and adjusted. But this should rarely happen in the heat of battle. When calm presides, parents and children can negotiate rules.

Some of this discussion about children's terrorist tactics may seem to dishonor Latter-day Saints' unique belief that children are born innocent (see Doctrine and Covenants 93:38). While we cherish the understanding that children do not come with the taint of original sin, we also understand that a fallen world can progressively poison them. "And the Lord spake unto Adam, saying: Inasmuch as thy children are conceived in [a world of] sin, even so when they begin to grow up, sin conceiveth in their hearts, and they taste the bitter, that they may know to prize the good" (Moses 6:55).

Children are born innocent, but a fallen world works furiously to teach them fallen ways. Our parenting can feed the natural child or nourish the child of Christ. Teaching law in a context of love is the way to do the latter.

2. Be Proactive

There is a second thing we can do to be sure our children learn to respect law. It is called proactive parenting. It is the opposite of reactive parenting, which waits for problems to break out and then reacts with threats and punishments. Reactive parenting tosses us to and fro with every wind of family challenge and emotion. It raises our blood pressure while damaging children's spirits.

Proactive parenting involves planning ahead, whether for a trip to the store or a summer vacation or preparing for church. Returning to the grocery store example, before parents take children into a store, they are wise to consider what they want to have happen and how to make that more likely. There are ways to have peaceful trips. For example, young children might ride in the cart and keep the grocery list. They might check items off as they are found. They become proud helpers. A creative friend blows up a produce bag for her child and invites the child to play with it as they wend their way through the aisles. A parent can also make a child a food guardian: "Would you hold on to the sweet potatoes?" Children can be invited to name the colors of the produce. The possibilities for keeping children happy and engaged are limitless—if we plan ahead and tune in to their needs.

Somewhat older children might help parents find needed items. Nancy invites our young grandchildren to be "store troopers" and help her find items on her list (and protect her from Darth Vader). It keeps them busy, active, and happy. We can even invite their input on select decisions: "What vegetable would you like us to buy for dinner?" "Is there a new fruit you would like to try?" The proactive parent might set limits on decisions that could go off the rails, like which breakfast cereal to buy: "I'm looking for a healthy cereal to buy. Do you think we should get Cheerios or Shredded Wheat?"

When the child begs for Fruit Loops, we have an opportunity to use what we have learned about compassion. "I know you love those. You wish we could have them this week. Maybe we will buy some for our next holiday." The child will whine. You can repeat your statement with great earnestness. There is no need to become indignant and accusatory. We can show that we are absolutely determined to honor the limit—while being perfectly pleasant.

This underscores a vital truth of parenting: We do not require children's assent to act wisely. They may insist that death is imminent and only Fruit Loops will save them. We can say, "Wow, you really wish you could have Fruit Loops!" Wise parents are not any more afraid to have their children upset with them than God is that we are occasionally upset with Him. We can act in our children's best interests even when they wish we would cave into their immediate wishes.

3. Stay Tuned

Even God watches for compliance: "And the Gods watched those things which they had ordered until they obeyed" (Abraham 4:18). God might have issued a command and gone about other business. He did not. He gives directions and watches to see that all is done correctly.

In our frantic family lives, we often give directions to children and then rush to the next crisis. Often, children realize we are distracted, so they ignore our directives. When we do not stay tuned to make sure our directives are taken seriously, children learn that laws have meaning only on those rare occasions when parents happen to notice their noncompliance. Children learn we are not serious about the rules we make.

Inadvertently, we sometimes teach children that blessings come without effort, crops grow without work, and rules are made to be ignored. They do not learn the law of the harvest. "Be not deceived; God is not mocked: for whatsoever a man soweth, that shall he also reap" (Galatians 6:7)

In my experience, the consistency that matters most in parenting is the consistency between our words and actions. When we give directives we need to make sure they are taken seriously. Wise parents may decide to have fewer rules so they can enforce them more consistently. They know that casualness about law is bad for the soul.

Much of this chapter is focused on preventing problems with children. In the next chapter, we will describe three kinds of control used with children and suggest ways to control effectively.

Reflection and Application

1. Do you tend to be stronger at showing love or setting limits? How will you help your children to experience a balance of both? You may draw on your spouse's strengths or draw other people into your children's lives or try to develop more of the balancing strength yourself.

2. Have you established clear limits that you are willing to enforce? Try to think through limits in areas of conflict. Be sure the limits honor children's preferences and adult wisdom. Be prepared to enforce the limits that make sense.

Cutting the Cake

One evening a mother was busily preparing a birthday party for one of her adult friends. Unfortunately, she had not figured out how to manage her young children while getting things ready. She was overwhelmed with party preparations, and the children tended themselves.

As people began to arrive, the five-year-old daughter became focused on the beautifully decorated cake on the table. She reached out to get a finger-full. Her mother threatened, "Don't you dare touch that cake!" The little girl withdrew her hand, but not her interest. When Mom got busy with other preparations, the daughter snatched a section of cake. When Mom discovered the offense, she exploded, "I told you to leave that cake alone! Go to your room!"

This mother had good intentions, but she set her daughter up for failure. Mom might have moved the cake. She might have busied her daughter with a task. ("Would you help me put out the napkins and plates?") She might have provided the daughter a snack. She might even have cut the daughter a piece of cake. A very proactive parent might even have created a separate cake for the children to enjoy. But when we bark orders without attending to children's needs and interests, we guarantee there will be problems.

Chapter 9
Guidance—Better and Poor Kinds of Control

By kindness and pure knowledge.

Doctrine and Covenants 121:42

Often we do the wrong things in parenting because we have lost sight of our real objectives. We may react to children's "misbehavior" in order to:

- Stop the noise and confusion.
- Teach them a lesson.
- Make them suffer for misdeeds.
- Express our tiredness and frustration.

The objectives listed above don't have an honored place as parenting objectives. There is a higher purpose for parental guidance than administering justice. The ultimate purpose of good guidance is to teach children to use their agency well. This is a vital—and challenging—objective; it will not be accomplished without wise and consistent effort.

But our correction is not always wise or consistent. We sometimes react to our children's behavior only when our mood makes it annoying to us. Therefore, they never know when inappropriate behavior will be laughed at, ignored, scolded, or punished. The very same behavior can elicit vastly different responses based on our current state of irritation. This does not teach children to respect laws or lawgivers.

Our objective is higher than obedience alone. We don't merely want our children to follow our rules, though we are generally glad when they do. We want them to internalize standards so that when we are not around to govern them, their inner sense of right and wrong still is. We want them to develop inner standards of goodness. We want something far more than compliance—we want moral development. This requires a very different kind of parenting from "natural man" parenting.

THREE KINDS OF CONTROL

Research has shown that parents' attempts to control children can usually be divided into three categories.

Control by Power

The first type of control is power assertion or coercion. We can use force—including spanking, threats, rewards, and punishment—to control our children. This technique gets compliance as long as we have more power than our children and are present to exercise that power. But this technique does not effectively teach children an inner set of values, i.e., moral internalization or conscience.

As you might expect, the use of power results in undesirable outcomes. Children of parents who regularly use power assertion are more likely to be either passive or rebellious. Neither of those outcomes is desirable. We don't want children who surrender their agency to powerful others, and we don't want children who senselessly fight against authority. Yet those are the likely outcomes of using power to control children.

When we live by the sword, we die by the sword. Parental use of power also results in lower social competence and poorer moral development in children.

One very popular form of coercion involves shaming and scolding children. Some parents might suppose that scolding and shaming are acceptable ways of helping children understand when they are behaving irresponsibly. Sometimes we lose our temper and seize scolding as an expression of our frustration. Or we may think of this as the quickest way of letting our children know they are out of line. But let's consider scolding from our children's perspective. In the words of researcher and author Erik Sigsgaard:

> *Scolding and punishment frighten children. Their natural tendency when scared is to cling to their mother [or father], but she [or he] is the one doing the scolding, and in doing so she is pushing the child away from her. This causes additional anxiety, and the child is frustrated—unable to act on his or her natural impulses. The people who are supposed to shield the child from anxiety and comfort the child are instead the source of an anxiety from which the child can find no shelter. This means that repeated and/or severe scolding may damage the child's fundamental trust.*[1]

One of the unintended effects of scolding and other forms of punishment and coercion is that children feel lost. In a confusing and hostile world, they have no advocate or friend. It is no wonder that coercion is not generally effective as a control technique. Coercion does not respect children.

Control by Love Withdrawal

The second kind of control technique is called love withdrawal. This involves any action by parents that suggests they won't sustain relationships with children who act in certain ways. Heaping guilt on children can be one form of love withdrawal. Timeouts can also be experienced as love withdrawal if they communicate to children that their parents don't want anything to do with them based on their behavior.

Research shows that love withdrawal is neither consistently constructive nor destructive. But it can cause children to feel guilty and insecure. It does not reliably get compliance, and it does not encourage moral development. But the larger concern for Latter-day Saints is that love withdrawal focuses on emotional manipulation and does not teach children better ways to use their agency. Instead it teaches them to feel unsafe and unsure in their own lives and families.

Control by Induction

There is a third kind of control that is far more effective than power assertion or love withdrawal at helping children learn to use their agency wisely. Scholars sometimes call it induction, which is defined as actions by the parents that attempt to influence and persuade children to do what is right. It involves helping children understand the effect of their behavior on others and themselves. It provides explanations and reasons.

Parents who use induction are far more likely to have children who are socially competent, independent, able to control their impulses, and responsible. Perhaps most importantly, such children have better moral internalization—

they do what is right because it is right. They do not require guards and enforcers.

GOD'S KIND OF CONTROL

The first time I studied the scholarly definition of induction, I was amazed by how similar it is to what God has recommended as the process for influencing other people. I will use His words and add a little commentary in brackets to connect the doctrine to research and experience.

No power or influence can or ought to be maintained by virtue of the priesthood [or parenthood; in other words, we must not use power to remove agency and coerce compliance], only by persuasion, by long-suffering, by gentleness and meekness, and by love unfeigned; By kindness, and pure knowledge *[Wow! That is pure induction!] which shall greatly enlarge the soul without hypocrisy, and without guile— [Hmm. We are better off when we use respectful methods. Our souls are enlarged, and we are spared the pains of hypocrisy.]*

Reproving betimes with sharpness, when moved upon by the Holy Ghost [not when irritated and tired—only when directed by God's holy messenger]; and then showing forth afterwards an increase of love toward him whom thou hast reproved, lest he esteem thee to be his enemy;

That he may know that thy faithfulness is stronger than the cords of death. [YIKES! The child must know *the power of our commitment to them!]* (Doctrine and Covenants 121:41–44; emphasis added)

Notice that God recommends patient persuasion, humble kindness, authentic love, and heavenly knowledge. This is a tall order for humans! It seems God wants to stretch us earthly parents to be more like Him.

For lessons on parenting from the perfect parent, let's consider how God treated His slow-to-learn son, Elijah. God gave Elijah the power to do a mighty miracle on Mt. Carmel, and it was witnessed by the assembled house of Israel. But in spite of the miracle, Ahab and Jezebel refused to repent. Rather than push forward in God's service, Elijah collapsed in discouragement. Three times God listened to his complaint about the children of Israel. Three times God did not lecture His shortsighted son. God invited him to meet Him for a sit-down on Mount Horeb. When Elijah was prepared by the forty-day journey, God taught him a great object lesson with wind, earthquake, and fire. It was because of Father's utter calmness that Elijah was able to feel the contrast between the wild forces of nature and God's voice when the Spirit spoke. If Father had shouted an impassioned lecture about duty and power, Elijah might not have learned the vital lessons. It would have sounded too much like earthquake, wind, and fire. Instead, God calmly instructed His son when he was ready to learn.

PARENTING ON EARTH

What does godly parenting look like when enacted by imperfect, human parents? Where are we most likely to fail along the way?

We have a smart, energetic grandson whose energy exceeds his impulse control by a sizeable margin. Naturally he regularly bumps into life and people. When he, his sister, and I are playing basketball at our house, it is not very long before the boy will collide with his sister as he lunges for the ball. She goes sprawling and scrapes a hand or knee. The scrape combined with the surprise leaves her hurt and sad. If we want to teach the boy to play basketball without tackling his sister, what should we do?

If we favor coercive methods (or we are simply tired and frustrated), we may lecture the boy, punish him, tell him that he is through with basketball for the day, or remove privileges. All of these are likely to make him more resentful of parents rather than more mindful of his sister.

Love withdrawal takes a different approach. It might include one of those "I'm so disappointed in you" lectures. It might insist he go to his room for an extended period. It might even entail name-calling, suggesting that the son is a disappointment. This would make the boy more lonely rather than more considerate.

What does wise induction recommend? In a perfectly calm and cordial manner, I ask him to sit down nearby and think about what he needs to do differently. He sits. His sister and I play basketball for a couple of minutes. Then I go sit by my grandson. "Can you tell me what went wrong?" He immediately and naturally blames her: "She got in the way!"

I calmly say, "Why don't you take a couple more minutes to see if you can figure out what you need to do differently?" (After all, he does not need to do his sister's repenting.) A couple minutes later, I sit by him again. "Can you tell me what you did wrong?" Usually he is ready to repent and says something like "I dove for the ball and ran into Sister."

Induction invites children to consider the effects of their behavior on others. "Yeah. What was that like for Sister?"

"She got hurt."

"You're right. She got painful scrapes. We try to never hurt each other. What can you do differently?"

"I need to watch for her and not run into her."

"Would you be willing to do that?"

The boy sighs. "Yeah."

"Are you ready to try again?"

We go back to basketball without any insults, threats, or punishments. I know from experience that he will be reckless with his sister again at some point. When that happens we will repeat this procedure as many times as we need to. Children need more than one encounter with reason and compassion to learn those principles. Effective parenting takes time, consistency, and patience. It takes many sessions (more than seventy times seven!) of patient teaching.

Sometimes we try to show our love for our children by ignoring the rules. Maybe we ignore a reasonable bedtime to win the child's favor. That's not the way to teach the law of the harvest. It teaches anarchy. Induction is the key to teaching responsible behavior. But induction does not include lecturing, guilting, isolating, hurting, or punishing. It is lovingly shepherding a child's mind and heart toward understanding the consequences of his or her acts and the effect on others.

The next chapter will consider ways to bring heartfelt compassion, healthy nurturing, and wise guidance into beautiful harmony.

Reflection and Application

Think of a recent disciplinary encounter with a child that didn't go very well. Can you see how you could have used induction rather than power assertion or love withdrawal? How would you use induction to be effective with your child? What would you do to help him or her learn to be considerate of others?

Sara and the Vase

When Sara was about four years old, she saw one of our teenage foster children dusting items on the mantel. Sara was intrigued by the vase that was among those things. She asked her foster sister to hand it to her. The automatic reaction was "No! You're too little—you'll break it." Naturally this response did not satisfy Sara's interest in the vase. And it hurt her feelings.

Sara found her mother in the kitchen. Nancy was not aware of the vase discussion between Sara and her foster sister. Once again Sara made her request to hold the vase. Nancy did several brilliant and relationship-building things. First, she took Sara's hand as they headed into the living room and answered, "Sure, Sara. But did you know that vases are breakable? Would you mind climbing up on the sofa and I will bring the vase to you?" (If we have the child stand on the rock hearth while we nervously watch her handle the vase, we are only setting her up for failure.) Sara was glad to sit on the sofa. Nancy got the vase and did another brilliant thing: she handed the vase to Sara so she could feel its weight and texture. Sara had control of her experience. Then Nancy sat by Sara and talked with her about what she saw, about the markings on the vase, and about what it meant to the family. When Sara had held the vase long enough, she said, "Thanks, Mom." And Nancy replied, "Sure, dear. If you ever want to see the vase again, just come and get me." What Nancy did was more than politeness. The net effect was to strengthen a relationship and help a little person grow in knowledge and confidence, while respecting reasonable limits.[1]

Chapter 10
The Heavenly View of Parenting

See that all these things are done in wisdom and order.

Mosiah 4:27

The previous chapters in this series have detailed the key processes of effective parenting:

1. Be a Flourishing Person. When we are flourishing—vibrant, happy, and connected to God—we bring a peacefulness and goodness to our relationships with our children. It also opens us up to the inspiration of Heaven.

2. Have Compassion. When we have heartfelt compassion for our children, we humbly seek to understand their development, individuality, circumstances, and hearts. This prepares us to act wisely and in their best interests.

3. Nurture. When we wholeheartedly and wisely love our children, we offer them love, joy, and peace. We provide the ideal environment for them to develop toward godliness.

4. Guide. When our objective in guiding our children is to help them learn to use their agency well, we help them become strong, resilient, and sensible people. We teach them to listen to their own inner voices and guide their lives by eternal principles.

We can wisely manage parenting challenges by applying these four principles. For example, consider a child who is playing happily with his toys when a neighbor child stops by to ask if he can come out to play. You are fine with having the two children play together outside, but you have a rule that toys must be picked up before children go out to play. You have many options. Let's consider how various options honor or dishonor the four principles.

You might say, "You cannot go out and play. You have not put away your toys." That response honors lawfulness (one part of guidance), but shortchanges both compassion and nurture.

You might say, "Son, you may go outside to play if you promise to pick up your toys when you come back in." This response seems to honor compassion and nurture, but it sends an unhealthy message about rules. Ignoring rules is not a good evidence of love; rather, it shows our own insecurity and desire to win the goodwill of our children.

You might say, "Son, as soon as you put your toys away, you may go outside." This may be pretty close to a good solution, but I think it skimps on nurture. It can be stark and confrontational. The heart of nurturing is that we help children move toward goodness.

Consider the following possibility: "Would you like to go outside, Son?" This question may seem like a no-brainer. Yet even if the child is almost certain to affirm his interest, you have shown that you are tuned in to the key question: What is your desire? Let's assume the child expresses enthusiastic interest in going outside. You can say with gusto, "Won't that be fun? You start putting away the toys while I go get your shoes."

With this option we show respect for rules and accountability, but we also show regard for our child's heart and desires. A key point is that we add our energy in support of his interest. We might offer to help with putting away the toys or any other task that facilitates the accomplishment of the objective. However, if we are putting away the toys while the child heads for the door, we have not effectively taught responsibility. We should gladly help our children, but we must do not do their work for them.

You can see that all four of the core principles should be used together to provide balanced and effective parenting. The Lord tells us to "see that all these things are done in wisdom and order" (Mosiah 4:27).

AS CHILDREN MATURE

The same principles apply to parenting teens, but the application must respect their growing maturity. For example, when our son, Andy, was sixteen and asked for permission to go to Lake Chewacla on a forthcoming Friday with his soccer-team buddies, I asked him questions and involved him in making the decision.

"Tell me about the activity, Son."

Andy described eating, fun, and swimming.

"Do you feel good about the doings?"

"Sure, Dad. They're good guys."

"Is there anything you're worried about?"

"No." [Long pause.] "Well, some of the guys use marijuana, but I'm not interested so it won't be a problem."

There is a key point here. Andy has just been honest with me in disclosing some worrisome details. If I react to that information by immediately forbidding him to go, he will likely decide there is no benefit in being honest with me. In the future, he may feel the best course is to hold back any information I might not like. He may become deceptive. And then I would be continually suspicious of him. There is a better way.

"Do you see any problems with some of the guys using marijuana?" I asked.

"No. If I'm not using it, it shouldn't be a problem." Andy paused. "Do you see any problem, Dad?"

"Two potential problems come to mind. If the party is busted, the police may consider you to be guilty by association. Also, knowing the mischievousness of your friends, I could imagine some of them chopping marijuana up and slipping it into your salsa or brownies."

Andy laughed. "I'll be careful, Dad." He clearly wanted to go.

Fortunately, he was asking early in the week. I invited him to think about it. We could talk about it after we had both had time to reflect on the decision.

A day or two later, Andy reopened the discussion: "Dad, I guess I don't need to be at that party. Do you mind if I invite some of my friends to the house for food, music, and ziplining?" We were delighted to have them come. Our house became the drug-free party site.

By the way, we also learned the painful truth that there are no parents cool enough that their teenage kids want them hanging around when they have a party. We stayed in the background making salsa and cookies that were entirely free of marijuana.

What if Andy had thought it over and still wanted to go to the party? Parents cannot say yes to something they don't feel good about. But even though we have to say no to the request, we can still honor the principles of effective parenting. We can have a conversation that invites our teen to share his or her perspectives and desires. Instead of simply laying down the law, we involve the teen in a discussion (appropriate for his or her maturity level) that helps the teen learn how to make responsible decisions. If he or she still wants to do something to which you can't say yes, you explain—but do not negotiate— your decision to say no. And if you are able, you could seek an option that allows your teen to go in the direction of his or her desires in a safe and acceptable way. For example, in this case you could offer the opportunity to have his friends over to your house for a fun alternative event.

A side note: Nancy and I have had many foster children in our home over the years. We allowed some of them to go to parties where marijuana was used—even by them. The reason we let the children go was not because we did not care about them. We let them go because such parties were not the beach head for influencing them. Teens whose lives were filled with bad choices must be helped line upon line. We might start by encouraging church attendance, prayer, scripture reading, or different friendship choices. We are more interested in drawing Children toward the light than in driving them from the darkness. All things must be done in wisdom and order (see Mosiah 4:27).

God has commanded us to bring up our children in light and truth (see Doctrine and Covenants 93:40). Light and goodness must be accompanied by responsibility and consequences, just as responsibility and consequences must be balanced by light and goodness. And all things must be done in wisdom and charity.

THE OTHER PURPOSE OF PARENTING

Sometimes we focus on only one set of parenting outcomes: the effects on children. God is interested in that outcome. He is also interested in the effects on parents. Parenting is a significant and soul-stretching challenge. God has a purpose within those challenges. He wants us as parents to be changed, refined, and enlarged, even as we strive to grow our children. God knows that earthly parenting is ideal preparation for heavenly parenting. He wants us to join Him in His work of blessing His children.

Any sensible person will be daunted by the prospect of parenting in the way Father does. We all fall short. We are shortsighted, impatient, narrow-minded, self-serving, and limited. We regularly fail to act wisely and graciously. Yet God teaches us the process.

In characteristic manner, He gives us an impossible task— like building an enormous ark, crossing the raging Red Sea, or surviving a fiery furnace. God likes to challenge us beyond our capacity. He keeps hoping those types of challenges will cause us to turn to Him and draw on heavenly power. He wants us to experience His miraculous and transformative power.

If we were to paraphrase in modern terms the words of the Apostle Paul, who was an expert at challenges, he might have said: "I just love it when my weaknesses and inability are so conspicuous. I am thrilled when I am persecuted and tortured. It is in times of such extremity that my abundant weakness is outshone by God's great power and goodness. Such times testify most clearly of His amazing ability and willingness to give me strength and to rescue His children" (see 2 Corinthians 12:10).

Godly parenting is one of many things that is impossible for humans on their own, but is fully possible in partnership with God (see Matthew 19:26).

GOD PROVIDED INSTRUCTIONS

God teaches that we cannot succeed in parenting without the prescribed spiritual processes He has taught from the beginning of time. The process of drawing power from heaven is taught in the words of Moroni: "And if men come unto me I will show unto them their weakness. I give unto men weakness that they may be humble; and my grace is sufficient for all men that humble themselves before me; for if they humble themselves before me, and have faith in me, then will I make weak things become strong unto them" (Ether 12:27).

There is a reason the word "humble" shows up three times in Moroni's formula for growth. We must be humble. We must recognize our desperate need for God and throw ourselves on His merits, mercy, and grace. Self-sufficiency is the enemy of progress. Submission is the door to power.

We must have faith in Christ. There is no other name under heaven whereby we can be saved or whereby we can parent effectively. Christ set the perfect example, provided the glorious teachings, delivered the infinite Atonement, and continues to sustain us with His compassion and goodness.

THE PARENTING POWER OF AN EARNEST DISCIPLE

As Latter-day Saints, we talk often of the vital practices of family home evening, family prayer, and family scripture study. Yet sometimes we are tempted to consider these practices and others meant to help us spiritually guide our families as merely daily or weekly routines. We might even approach them with impatience ("It's so difficult to make the time!") or with condescension ("I'll do it for the kids, but only because we are supposed to").

As normal Latter-day Saints, we listen to the counsel of Church leaders in our Sunday meetings. We ponder guidance provided by scripture. We pray for heavenly guidance. But then we get swamped by the busyness and pressures of everyday family life. Perhaps we tend to view the directions we have received as not all that relevant to the press and challenges of day-to-day parenting.

God would have us think differently. What if we approached our role as parents with the heart of an earnest disciple? What if we actively invited Christ into our homes every day to partner with us in our parenting? How would that impact our homes and families?

Imagine a burdened single mom kneeling with her son by his bedside, pleading for God to help him find patience with his brother.

Imagine homes where the children love the characters in scripture because those characters have been their companions at the breakfast table or at bedtime or whenever scripture stories have been regularly read and celebrated.

Imagine homes where children hear their parents in family prayer express great love for God and plead for His mercy in their homes and lives.

Imagine families gathered around the dinner table on the Sabbath, sharing their best experiences of the day or discussing what each family member most remembers from their worship experience and classes. Imagine family members united in awe as they witness God blessing and teaching each of them in perfectly customized ways.

Imagine families where repentance is taught powerfully by parents who willingly acknowledge their shortcomings, ask forgiveness of those offended, and seek earnestly to be more Christlike, where children are taught by their parents' example that mistakes are not tragedies when the Atonement is applied.

Imagine family home evenings where parents tell great stories of their ancestors and the way their devotion has opened the gates of eternity. Imagine families where every member feels the love and support of departed ancestors.

Imagine children who understand that regardless of the trials and disappointments they experience, they can still "be of good cheer" and appreciate their blessings because they witness their parents' firm conviction that the Lord is with them always (see Doctrine and Covenants 68:6).

Imagine homes in which children learn faith, compassion, charity, forgiveness, service, joy, and a love for the Lord because those principles are the foundation of their family.

Being a godly parent is much more than simply participating in a checklist of vital practices or following the latest parenting recommendations from Pinterest. Incredible power is available to us as parents when we have the heart of an earnest disciple and when we partner with Jesus.

I conclude this chapter with the inspired and inspiring words of President Ezra Taft Benson:

Would not the progress of the Church increase dramatically today with an increasing number of those who are spiritually reborn? Can you imagine what would happen in our homes? . . .

The world would mold men by changing their environment. Christ changes men, who then change their environment. The world would shape human behavior, but Christ can change human nature. . . .

You do change human nature, your own human nature, if you surrender it to Christ. Human nature has been changed in the past. . . . And only Christ can change it. . . .

Yes, Christ changes men, and changed men can change the world. Men changed for Christ will be captained by Christ. . . . Finally, men captained by Christ will be consumed in Christ. . . .

Their will is swallowed up in his will. They do always those things that please the Lord. Not only would they die for the Lord, but, more important, they want to live for Him.

Enter their homes, and the pictures on their walls, the books on their shelves, the music in the air, their words and acts reveal them as Christians. They stand as witnesses of God at all times, and in all things, and in all places. They have Christ on their minds, as they look unto Him in every thought. They have Christ in their hearts as their affections are placed on Him forever.[2]

God invites us to be filled with Christ and His perfect doctrine, principles, and power so we may be saved along with our dear ones.

Reflection and Application

Try it. Imagine your family in the ways described in this chapter. In those areas where the hoped-for performance seems hopelessly beyond reach, pray for heavenly mercy and patiently do all you are able to do.

Poopy

Dear and wise friends were struggling with their four-year-old son, who liked to scandalize his older sisters by occasionally blurting out the word "poopy." This was an especially big problem since the girls were so earnest about doing what was right. When the boy shot out the word, the sisters became indignant and ran to the parents, who tried all the usual things to get their son to modify his vocabulary. Nothing worked.

The parents realized that what they were doing was not working. Rather than amp up the pressure on the son, they chose to consider why he was saying the word. They realized that his amazing sisters were praised often and generously for their many accomplishments. He, the younger brother, had neither the patience nor the maturity to compete with them on their ground. Using an inflammatory word was a guaranteed way for him to get attention. It kept the family in an uproar.

The parents wisely decided to do two things: decrease the attention from them and the siblings on the offending word, and provide added opportunities for the boy to shine. It took only a matter of days before "poopy" disappeared from the boy's vocabulary.

Chapter 11

A Problem-Solving Guide:
Applying Godly Parenting to the
Continuing Challenges of Parenting

The doctrine of the priesthood shall distill upon
thy soul as the dews from heaven.

Doctrine and Covenants 121:45

We all feel divided at times, frustrated and torn by specific parenting dilemmas. We feel an impulse to act in one way, but we have a nagging uncertainty: "Am I really doing (or planning to do) the right thing?" Other times, we simply don't know what to do. That feeling of perplexity is one of the burdens of parenting.

This chapter is not primarily about how to deal with life's little dramas, like a child who forgets to put his socks away or spills her milk. This chapter is intended to help you with patterns that start to hold a relationship hostage. Maybe we are regularly sharp or impatient with one child. Or maybe we feel that a child is contrary or rebellious. Or maybe we're worried that a child is irresponsible.

This chapter is about those problems that keep recurring. I want to suggest a way to deal with those knotty difficulties according to the pattern described in previous chapters about godly parenting.

Think of a parenting challenge you have been wrestling with. Maybe you have continuing tension in your relationship with one child. Or maybe you worry about the decisions of another. Close your eyes and revisit times when you've felt a concern about one of your children. Have that situation in mind as you work through these five sections.

STEP 1: BE A FLOURISHING PERSON

When we are unhappy, frustrated, angry, confused, aimless, and empty, we don't do our best work as parents. While we may not be in such extreme places very often, even small doses of unhappiness (or stress or frustration) can get in the way of effective parenting. We've all experienced that.

Before we make big parenting decisions or before dealing with big parenting challenges, we need to get our minds and hearts right. (Actually, before we make even small parenting decisions, we need to get our minds and hearts right.) So we start not by focusing on the child and the problem, but by focusing on God. In a sense, the key question here is just what Alma asked: "If ye have experienced a change of heart, and if ye have felt to sing the song of redeeming love, I would ask, can ye feel so now?" (Alma 5:26).

There are really two parts to Alma's question:

1. Have you ever felt that soul-filling love of God that makes us sing with joy?
2. Do you have that same feeling right now?

If you have never felt that love, the first order of business is to discover it. I encourage you to find something that lifts your spirits. Maybe it is a piece of beautiful music, a scriptural passage, a general conference talk, an inspiring book, or a great story. Let yourself be engulfed by that message. As our spirits soar, the veil is thin. It is then that we are most likely to feel God wrap us in His arms. Nothing is as powerful or as life-changing as feeling His love.

Many of us have felt His love repeatedly trying to break into our lives, but we resist it. "You can't love me when I do so many stupid things!" I encourage you to drop your defenses against God. Do the things that lift your spirits and thin the veil for you. Let Him grab you with His love. Or just stop resisting His entreaties. Let your perfect Father have you. He changes everything. He give us purpose, hope, meaning, energy, and direction. After all, He and Jesus Christ are the Light and Life of the world. They are also the Light and Life of every individual soul—including mine and yours.

Alma's second question is whether the experience of God's love is real and present in our souls *right now*. We should not enter into the sacred and delicate business of difficult parenting without being armed with the love of God. We cannot deal with difficulties unless that fire is burning within us right now.

So, before undertaking any problem-solving venture, fill yourself with that love. Let any troubles be "swallowed up in the joy of Christ" (Alma 31:38). If you cannot get to such a place of joy right now, put off the problem-solving self-dialogue until you can. Do not try to solve eternal problems with puny mortal tools. Wait. Wait until you feel God's love burning in your heart.

Do not grieve the Spirit by rushing into battle unarmed with "the breastplate of righteousness and your feed shod with the preparation of the gospel of peace; Above all, taking the shield of faith, wherewith ye shall be able to quench all the fiery darts of the wicked" (Ephesians 6:14–16).

The surest sign that we are filled with the love of God is feeling loving toward the people in our lives—even the annoying ones. Do you feel loving toward the child who is currently confusing or frustrating you? When you feel God's love and goodness coursing through you, you are ready to solve the problems that burden your family. You are ready to thwart Satan and empower goodness.

Reflection and Application

Are you feeling peaceful and assured in the love of God so that you are prepared to solve the parenting problems that burden you? If not, what will activate that love in your life? If so, move on to the next steps.

STEP 2: HAVE COMPASSION

Let's assume you have thought of a specific parenting challenge you are dealing with. You are probably very familiar with your logic in the conflict. You may have spent hours thinking about a child's bad behavior and what it means about his or her character (or lack thereof). You may have even worried about the long-term consequences for a child who would act that way. "Is my child on the path to destruction, immorality, rebellion, apostasy, criminality . . .?" We fret and blame.

But half of the story tends to get neglected: the child's side. We know our perceptions, our concerns, our indignation, but we may not fully know or understand the child's story. What is life like for him or her? What is he or she worried about, burdened by, hurt by? What are the child's concerns and life challenges?

What might my child be trying to tell me with this behavior? Maybe the child is saying, "I need to feel respected by you. I need you to engage in a discussion with me and try to understand me." Or the child may be saying, "You keep changing your mind and you're making me crazy!" Or the child may be saying something entirely different. But when we can get out of our own concerns and complaints and try to walk a day in the child's shoes, we may get vital information about what he or she truly wants.

There are a lot of sensible reasons children do what they do. They may feel tired, sick, or lonely. They may not know any better. They may be afraid, stressed, or anxious. They may want to feel accepted by their friends. They may want to draw us into their lives. They may be desperate for our love and attention.

Here is a key concept to remember: children do what they do for reasons that make sense to them. When their actions do not make sense to us, it is not because they are bad or crazy; it is because we don't yet understand them. I am not suggesting that children always have good reasons for what they do, but they do have reasons that make sense to them. When we understand their reasons, their logic, and their objectives, we will be better able to help them.

It may be helpful to discuss the child and the conflict with another person who loves that child. The insight of another person can enrich our understanding. But, of course, compassion is more than understanding why the child does as he or she does. Compassion includes feeling his or her struggle and pain. That alone is challenging. But if that compassion is to be effective, we must communicate it. Somehow we need to show our children we are touched by their struggles and pain, by the feeling of their infirmities (see Hebrews 4:15).

So, this foundation for solving our parenting problems involves both understanding our children's perspectives and showing them that we care. To communicate your compassion, I encourage you to use statements that focus on your children and their feelings. It is not the use of "you" or "I" that matters as much as the focus of the message.

- "I'm trying to understand and find words to describe your feeling."
- "You must be tired of that."
- "You wonder if it will ever work out."
- "Did you feel humiliated?"
- "I bet you wish things were different."

It is only when the child feels valued and understood that real negotiation can take place. It will not work to get a resolve to do better and then swoop in with announcements of new plans and programs. The foundation for building a new pattern involves the development of genuine compassion.

Stephen R. Covey tells a meaningful story about a colleague who sought his advice for dealing with a teenage son who was resentful and distant. The father had tried to talk with his son, but every conversation degenerated into an angry dad and a defensive son. Covey advised him to listen to his son and show understanding. The man insisted that he had, but his son was stubborn and unreasonable. (It is hard for us humans to take responsibility for our own problems!) The father finally got desperate and humble enough to apologize sincerely to his son for his mistakes. The father began to really listen. His compassion opened the door to real conversation and a renewed relationship.[1]

Reflection and Application

Do you feel genuine compassion for your child and the challenges he or she faces? Do you have the words to show your compassion? Are you willing to stick with compassion even when your child is prickly?

STEP 3: NURTURE

Once we are feeling peaceful and compassionate, we are ready to craft the message of love that will help the child feel personally valued.

While we may deeply love our children, there are times when irritation and frustration block the sense of affection and appreciation that are essential to the relationship. We don't have the right to correct anyone we don't love. Only heartfelt love gives us the right to be in a person's life and the right to influence him or her.

When we want to cover up our mistakes, prove we are right, or control another person, we have no power (see Doctrine and Covenants 121:34–37). Power comes from love. But a different kind of power comes from love. It is not the kind of power that compels action; it is the kind of power that invites shared growth.

Once we are feeling peaceful and compassionate (steps 1 and 2 in this process), we are ready to craft the message of love that will help the child feel personally valued.

In parenting we often keep the focus firmly fixed on irritations. "Why can't you ever . . . ?" "When will you learn . . .?" We seem to assume that the way to improve children is driving them out of their misdeeds and misbehavior. That doesn't work.

Consider God's process. He starts by loving us. In fact, "we love him because he first loved us" (1 John 4:19). He wins our hearts with his love and goodness. Of course it is worth noting that His love does not make Him surrender to our tantrums. While He loves us with all His heart, He unfailingly honors law.

Consider a paraphrase of Haim Ginott's words: "It is said that nature always sides with the hidden flaw. Parents have the opposite role: to side with the hidden asset, to minimize a child's deficiencies, intensify his experience, and enlarge his life."[2]

The spirit of irritation must not be the governing principle as we work with our children. Quite the contrary. We can only solve problems and grow heavenward when we are filled with love for them.

Rather than focus on the problems we're trying to solve, nurture invites us to focus on the goodness in our children—on their finest moments, their greatest qualities, and their purest intentions. As we fill our hearts with love for them, we are prepared to solve problems in the Lord's way.

Reflection and Application
1. What do you love best about your child? What have been some of your finest moments? What are the qualities of heart and character that you admire in the child?
2. Can you see the reasons your child does the things he or she does? How do the actions make sense from the child's perspective?

STEP 4: GUIDE

The enormous challenge in guidance is to remember its purpose. It is not about making children pay for mistakes but about helping them learn from experience. And there is a vast difference between those two objectives. We are likely to be confused about the difference unless we have peace, compassion, and love in our hearts.

Proper guidance is filled with God's trademark goodness. It is He who has commanded us to bring up our children in light and truth. It is He whose creativity is filled with lilting goodness.

Rather than hearts filled with a shriveled "no!" we can have hearts that are filled with a bigger, more gracious "yes!" Rather than lecture (and insult) our children about their forgetfulness, we can make a game out of turning off the lights, closing the doors, *and* picking up socks. Rather than get angry when a child leaves his bike on the lawn, maybe we scoop him up in our arms and ask him to solve the mystery of the mislaid bike. Rather than ground children until the end of time, maybe we invite them to help us find solutions to our chronic differences.

Sure, there will be consequences. There will be groundings. There will be lost privileges. But the focus must be on teaching, strengthening, and improving. The best guidance leads to better actions and closer relationships.

When we find ourselves defending a disciplinary action, when we find ourselves feeling tense and defensive, there is a good chance we have acted under the influence of anger and the prince of darkness. Effective guidance brings light.

Admittedly, children will sometimes be quite unhappy with the limits and restrictions that will be necessary. But we would never burn down a temple just to fry an egg (to paraphrase the famous statement[3]), and we would not sacrifice the long-term growth of a child just for immediate peace and goodwill.

Once, a sweet mother asked me for counsel in dealing with her three-year-old son, who had suddenly become crazy every time she vacuumed the floor. She was a kind and compassionate person, but she wondered if the only solution was punishing the boy. I asked her what was happening in their family life. Mom was vacuuming more often since she had an infant who was starting to play on the floor. In fact, she was vacuuming at least once a day instead of the usual weekly routine. We cannot know exactly what the new vacuuming regimen meant to the three-year-old. Maybe it seemed to him that every time he started to play, the vacuum came after him.

I suggested she discuss a vacuuming schedule with her son. Maybe he preferred that she vacuum when he was gone to a neighbor's house. Maybe she could just alert him and he would retire to his room while she vacuumed. Maybe he could help her vacuum. She had the discussion with her son and they settled on a vacuuming schedule. His outbursts disappeared.

Not every problem will follow this pattern. But every parenting challenge can be properly addressed with compassion, nurture, and wise guidance. We must be careful that we do not wield parenting power recklessly. Power may gain compliance when children are small, but it generates resentment that bubbles up in adolescence.

When God taught the great sermon about power (see Doctrine and Covenants 121), He described two preconditions to godly power:

- "Let thy bowels also be full of charity toward all men, and to the household of faith" (v. 45).
- "And let virtue garnish thy thoughts unceasingly" (ibid).

What happens when we are filled with charity and see the good in our children? "Then shall thy confidence wax strong in the presence of God; and the doctrine of the priesthood [or parenting power] shall distil upon thy soul as the dews from heaven" (ibid).

But that is not all. God offers blessings that extend into eternity: "The Holy Ghost shall be thy constant companion, and thy scepter an unchanging scepter of righteousness and truth; and thy dominion shall be an everlasting dominion, and without compulsory means it shall flow unto thee forever and ever" (v. 46).

Reflection and Application

As you consider a relationship that has often challenged you, can you see a way to focus on loving and teaching rather than battling and punishing? How can you be more effective in teaching the law of the harvest in the spirit of love and encouragement?

STEP 5: HAVE AN ETERNAL PURPOSE

Part of the challenge of parenting is that we are repeatedly blindsided by problems. We are marching merrily through life when a child punches his sister or spills her drink. We are doing well until we are hijacked by life's wacky fallenness.

But this is no accident; it is quite by design. C. S. Lewis puts this in perspective:

> *When I come to my evening prayers and try to reckon up the sins of the day, nine times out of ten the most obvious one is some sin against charity; I have sulked or snapped or sneered or snubbed or stormed. And the*

excuse that immediately springs to my mind is that the provocation was so sudden and unexpected; I was caught off my guard, I had no time to collect myself. . . . Surely what a man does when he is taken off his guard is the best evidence for what sort of man he is? Surely what pops out before the man has time to put on a disguise is the truth? If there are rats in a cellar you are most likely to see them if you go in very suddenly. But the suddenness does not create the rats: it only prevents them from hiding. In the same way the suddenness of the provocation does not make me an ill-tempered man; it only shows me what an ill-tempered man I am. The rats are always there in the cellar, but if you go in shouting and noisily they will have taken cover before you switch on the light. Apparently the rats of resentment and vindictiveness are always there in the cellar of my soul.[4]

While cool, polite, steady social environments do not test the deeper layers of our character, family life does. It is there that we get the challenges that make us angry more than anywhere else.

God gave us family life so we could have plenty of practice at keeping an eternal perspective. Family life invites us to sacrifice our convenience and preferences in order to bless people who are still learning. Parenting regularly stretches us toward godliness.

Our Partner in the Process

We must be very careful about our strategy for reforming our parenting. We simply cannot remake our own characters. As C. S. Lewis reminded us: "After the first few steps in the

Christian life we realise that everything which really needs to be done in our souls can be done only by God."[5]

Thus we learn, in the great scriptural pattern, to constantly call upon God for mercy:

Have mercy that I may be filled with Thy goodness.

Have mercy that I may properly value the children Thou hast given me.

Have mercy that I may know their hearts.

Have mercy that I may be a messenger of Thy love.

Have mercy that I may have the wisdom and patience to teach well.

Have mercy that my soul may be reformed in Thy image.

Have mercy and change my heart and my family.

Through His mercy, we can be changed by His grace. With His help—His love, His nurturing kindness, His guidance for us—we can love, nurture, and guide our families in His way.

May God bless you on your parenting journey.

Reflection and Application

1. Can you see the whole of your child—the radiant spirit that came from God's presence and the glorious person ultimately perfected by God?

2. Do you recognize that even the biggest problems with your child may be a manifestation of keen sensitivity or a strong

spirit? Will you seek a way to honor that strength and point it toward wiser use?

3. Can you see yourself as a heavenly parent in training? Do you sense how much God wants to help you as you partner with Him in perfecting His children? Do you feel His love and compassion for you as you keep learning and trying?

Notes

Chapter 1

1. Charles A. Smith, Dorothea Cudaback, H. Wallace Goddard, and Judy Myers-Walls. *The National Extension Parent Education Model* (Manhattan, KS: Kansas State University, 1994).

Chapter 2

1. Martin Seligman, *Authentic Happiness* (New York City: Free Press, 2002).

Chapter 3

1. Story facing chapter 3: *Ensign,* Mar. 1983, 63. Reprinted with permission.
2. www.thefreedictionary.com.
3. John W. Welch, "The Good Samaritan: A Type and Shadow of the Plan of Salvation," *BYU Studies* (Provo, UT: Brigham Young University, 1999), 38(2): 81.
4. Ibid.
5. Haim G. Ginott, *Between Parent and Teenager* (New York City: Macmillan Co., 1969), 52–53. Name in story has been modernized.
6. Ibid, 53–55.
7. Ginott, *Between Parent and Child, The Bestselling Classic That Revolutionized Parent-Child Communication,* revised and updated edition, ed. Alice Ginott and H. Wallace Goddard (New York City: Three Rivers Press, 2003), 6.
8. Joseph Smith, *Teachings of the Prophet Joseph Smith,* comp. Joseph Fielding Smith (Salt Lake City, UT: Deseret Book Co., 1938), 241.

Chapter 4

1. Story facing chapter 4: adapted from H. Wallace Goddard, *Modern Myths and Latter-day Truths* (CreateSpace, 2009).
2. Brigham Young, *Discourses of Brigham Young,* comp. John A. Widtsoe (Salt Lake City, UT: Deseret Book Co., 1954), 207.
3. Kauro Yamamoto, O. R. Davis, Stanislaw Dylak, Jean Whittaker, Colin Marsh, and P. C. van der Westhuizen. "Across Six Nations: Stressful Events in the Lives of Children," *Child Psychiatry and Human Development,* 26(3) (1996): 139–50.

Chapter 5

1. Story facing chapter 5: Goddard, *Finding Joy in Family Life* (Joymap, 2008).
2. Ginott, *Between Parent and Teenager,* 65–66.
3. Ibid, 70.
4. John Gottman with Joan DeClaire, *Raising an Emotionally Intelligent Child* (New York City: Simon & Schuster, 1997), 76–100.
5. Ibid, 94.

Chapter 7

1. Story facing chapter 7: adapted from Goddard, *Finding Joy in Family Life.*

Chapter 8

2. Story facing chapter 8: adapted from ibid.

Chapter 9

1. Erik Sigsgaard, *Scolding: Why It Hurts More than It Helps* (New York City: Teachers College Press, 2005), 143.

Chapter 10

1. Story facing chapter 10: adapted from Goddard, *Finding Joy in Family Life.*
2. Ezra Taft Benson, "Born of God," First Presidency Message, *Ensign,* July 1989.

Chapter 11

1. Stephen R. Covey, *The 7 Habits of Highly Effective Families* (New York City: Golden Books, 1997), 13–14.
2. Ginott, *Teacher and Child: A Book for Parents and Teachers* (New York City: Macmillan, 1972), 179.
3. Hugh B. Brown attributed the expression to Dr. Henry A. Bowman: "No really intelligent person will burn a cathedral to fry an egg, even to satisfy a ravenous appetite" (Hugh B. Brown, *The Abundant Life* [Salt Lake City: Bookcraft, 1965], 67).
4. C. S. Lewis, *Mere Christianity* (New York: HarperCollins, 1952), 192–93.
5. Ibid, 193.

Recommended Resources

The best guides in family matters are the sacred scriptures, the softening and enlightening influence of the Holy Ghost, and the inspired pronouncements of the brethren.

There are surprisingly few great books on parenting. As recommended earlier, Haim G. Ginott's *Between Parent and Child* is the classic on showing compassion while setting limits. This wise approach is further discussed in John Gottman's *Raising an Emotionally Intelligent Child.*

The quality of your marriage has a big impact on the quality of your parenting. There are several excellent books on marriage. For a spiritual perspective, my *Drawing Heaven into Your Marriage* may be helpful. From a secular perspective, consider Gottman's *The Seven Principles for Making Marriage Work.*

Many sensible and grounded resources are available through Cooperative Extension. I encourage you to go to: www.arfamilies.org for programs that my colleagues and I developed on personal well-being, marriage, and parenting. All are based on the best research and the contents are available to you free of charge.

About the Author

In his writing, H. Wallace (Wally) Goddard, PH.D., uniquely combines scholarship, faith in the gospel of Jesus Christ, and sheer joy. He received his doctorate in family and human development and is currently a professor of family life for the University of Arkansas Cooperative Extension. In this position, Wally develops programs on well-being, marriage, and parenting. He has written numerous books for LDS, general, and professional audiences and has served on national committees on parenting and marriage. He has served in the LDS Church as a bishop, high councilor, and institute teacher. He describes his wife, Nancy, as the most peaceful and charitable parent he knows. Wally and Nancy have three adult children and a growing number of amazing grandchildren.